The Living Incantation of Black Life

by

Shiyon Perriyon

Created in the Essence

First Edition

ISBN: 978-0-7596-4449-6 (*e*)
ISBN: 978-0-7596-4450-2 (*sc*)

This book is printed on acid free paper.

First published by Urban Farmer Publishing

Cover Art by the Urban Farmer Design Team.

Urban Farmer Publishing is a subsidary
of 2001 Urban Farmer Entertainment
The Urban Farmer Collective
Detroit, Michigan U.S.A.

Catalog No. UF-00001-A

1stBooks – rev. 11/1/01

A

Perriyon

Presentation

A

URBAN FARMER

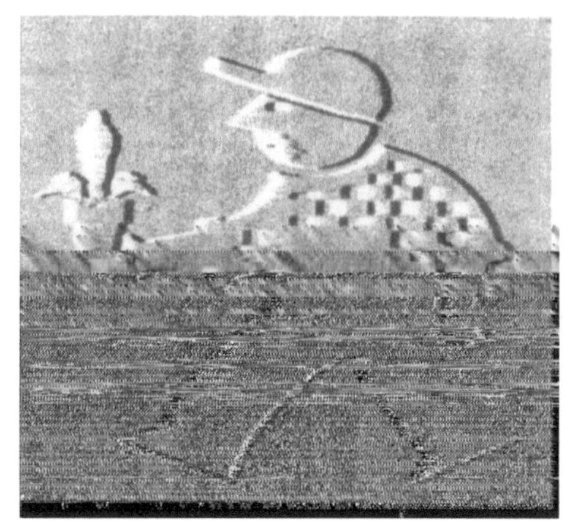

PRODUCTION

Table of Content

MYSELF (Part One)

To My Brothers (Part One)

To My Sisters (Part One)

To the 1 you Love

To the Father of Creation and his vision of Life (Part One)

The First Book of Shiyon and The Celestial Psalms of I BE

Five Day's in the Hole (Written in Ghetto Slang)

Thank's to You

The new Century has arrived with
a ever moving force of Creativity
Madd Respect for the
Creative forces of
Erykah Badu
Lauryn Hill
Maxwell
Common
D'Angelo
The Roots
Jill Scott
Q-tip
Babyface
Kelly Price
R. Kelly
Donell Jones
Musiq the Soulchild
Jessica Care Moore
Dead Prez
Mos Def
KRS One
Jay Z
To every hood and ghetto
To every ear that listens
and understands,
The souls of Black Folks

The Moment of Awakening

The point of understanding a world around you, so small that it sucludes you in a state of lonesome sorrow, and a world so large that you a look out into a endless vision of souls and emotions, looking into the eyes of living beings. Connecting with the world through tragidy and suffering, bonding with the tears that roll down the cheeks of the sad and afflicted.

A world so unorganized and filled with turmoil. A world searching through the dead-end road of diplomacy for the answers to questions of peace. When they should be searching the essence of within for the unity and communion living.

Endlessly the supply of emotions and understandings of emotions swallow your thoughts like a open well in the seam of living. Watching the reactions of living beings as they respond to the emotions that govern the human race.

I am the writer of the times, the ghetto times, the times of sin, the times of Jesus, the times of pain, and the times of joy. I am the writer of life, from the good life, to the bad life.

I am the writer of emotions, from the sadness that swells in our heart to the happiness that flows from your soul. I am the jealousy that tears lives apart, I am the hatred that grows in your heart. I am the writer of expression, expressing the inner most questions that you yearn to ask but fear that no one will understand. I express the answers that you seek in search of the reasons of life. I am your guide through the belly of life, I am Shiyon Perriyon the Living incantation of Black Life.

Myself
(Part One)

MYSELF

I am inhuman,
Abstract yet finite,
creativity is my breath
Infinity, my soul
I see what others cannot see
I feel what other only dream of feeling.
My mental abilities are as deep as
the great oceans upon the earth,
and reach as far as the uncharted regions
of all time and space in the universe.
To attempt to look in my mind may cause
you to fall into a deep world of illusion and mystery
that you may never return from.
Or would you really want to.

A Master
(Shadow Side)

**A master at the taste of a woman's flesh, so sweet so petite
oh my I love you so. The things you do the things
you say can only be done in your sexy sway. Hmmm I see the way
you bend and move ever so slow in my view, believe
me my dear, I love you.**

I Love Detroit, MI
(MoTown-Hitsville U.S.A.)

I Love where I'm from
the home of Hitsville U.S.A.
The place on the map that says,
this is where it's at.
A city of power and Gordy.
Franklin speaking, the city that
Miracles you with it's Knights and Pipes,
made you be Gaye with Terrell in Holland, Dozier, Holland
with the Fantastic Fourand the All-Stars.
It must be in the waters Wells that's turning us into
a Starr times 5.
Then like commodores we showed you Wonders, Marvelettes
And Reeves with Vandella's
It made you Tops and as Perriyon rides around in his Contours,
people say thank God for the Temptations to be Supremes
Yes this is where I'm from.
and as I stand here on Mighty West Grand Blvd,
I say I love where I'm from.
Detroit, MI

Mary Jane

Intimately I approach the domain forbidden,
A land of illegal pleasures, and false feelings,
and it feels good.
I have never done this before but this night I tried,
The smoke thick and white pouring into my lungs like a waterfall.
This little brown stick with orange hair, makes my world move in slow motion everytime I kiss it.
We all call it Mary Jane and she never let's you down
she's always on time.
She never complains, she never say's no.
But she's a freak, she loves me to suck on her tail, it makes her feel good to be in control.
That why I love her.
She makes me write the illest, realist shit.

Blue to Grey
Let my tears go Away

**A land full of golden groves and leafmeal,
I fall into a daze of a sky so bright,
As the sun beams through the trees I see flickering
simultaneously as magnificent specticals of light.
I watch as my eyes are filled with a shower of stars
and my arms reach for the warm rays as shinny as gold,
then when I reach that peak.
My blue sky turns grey and my world becomes meak.
And as the warm rays leave and rain begans to fall,
It washes away my wishes and all my dreams are gone.**

In the Essence of Eternity

I walk intimatly through the trees of a large green blanket,
With the sun seeping through the cracks like small glowing jewels upon my face,
take me,
I ask the wood how do you feel and what stories could you tell me of eternity,
I know you know,
Speak to me of the treasures that span from here to the beginning of time,
Tell me of species that don't exist anymore, how were they?
Were they beautiful?
If I knew your language, my God the things that i could learn,
I am fascinated by your wisdom, you great antient observer,
Astonishing.

SADNESS

What justifies pain?
I don't know. Do you?
Can you tell me what it is?
Like a blind man all I see is darkness, because colors and eyes
so bright have no place where I live.
All that lives here is eyes of water dripping like rain
squeezed out of two swollen spheres.
Like the weather a beautiful sunny day becomes a raging storm
of black clouds, grey skies, and oceans falling.
You can see the pain dragging me down to the ground,
everytime I see you. I can't
explain how I feel. Spill my love on the floor I have it no more you do.
You hunted my heart, you slaughtered it, you can mend it,
I would love you to, if you can justify pain.
Who can I run to? Where can I go?
I am alone with no home because home is where the
heart is and my heart is gone.
Sometimes love can be as hard as a diamond and sometimes
as soft as a birds feathers.
So tell me what justifies pain?

Your Choice

Together we can have peace,
Seperated we can have war.

Together we can love,
Seperated we can hate.

Together we can hold hands,
Seperated we can hold weapons.

Together we can be free,
Seperated we can be enslaved.

Shadows

What is it behind you?
What is it on the side of you?
Your darkness shows your light, for your light is formed by your night.
Cause when the world dims your light the dark side takes control and in your darkness you can understand the need of your light.

Your love for it

Your heart is your soul connection to anything you do.
No matter how much teaching and learning you have achieved.
It does not matter unless you have understanding.
the understanding that no matter if your the President of the United States or a bumb in the streets,
It's the love you have for it that makes you do it at all.

The Picture

So sensual the gold that gleams with horrific light
as the shades of black enrich themselves in it's spacious plains.

The blues dark and light enraptured by their every touch
within a eclair of majesty.

Let your mind flow as the colors dance in a meadow of forever.

They social and ballroom across the picture so sweet and so soft.
Tender as a child yet as strong as a force of nature.

Say Goodnight to the World

Night Express,
suggestions are apparent,
life is hard, life is devious,
it can destroy young minds.
I found a way out within the world of the rhyme.
Notes echo,
words soar,
my mind excells.
Emotions are all around running wild.
Can you see them?
It hurts, it brings joy, what will it bring next.
Fame, sorrow, money, failure, I am all that it is and all it can be.
We are dead with our eyes open, so I try to give support to all in the hood.
Because it's hared and I'll be back with all my love and all my heart.
Goodnight to the World

Expression One

Her bones may now rest,
Her womb shall forever sleep,
The eyes that once saw good and bad,
Shall see no more,
The lips that once spoke in all emotions,
Shall speak no more,
for she is born again as the soul,
Pure as a Genesis,
Her better place is at hand,
And acknowledged.

Expression Five

Pain is hurt timed by eternity and divided by love and happiness.
For those who laugh the most hides the most pain cause they hold it in.
And those who laugh a little hides small pain for they fight it and those who inflict pain and hurt may as well destroy himself or beg for forgiveness.
And those who endured pain of others may become blessed by the heaven.

Expression Sixteen

Why do your eyes cut me, looking straight through me

as if their is something you want to see.

You don't really know what your looking for do you.

You don't know what your getting yourself into

looking into the soul of a vampire.

At times as cold as a day in december,

and at other times as seductive as the sweetest ballad created.

The Enlightenment of the Disciple

Fatih is the enlightenment of a world that was and soon shall be again. God made the forest and the rivers that flows through them. The wolf became the most cunning and relentless hunter in the forest and so the symbol was born.
From the sky the light fell,
three bright onyx's in the middle of the night and brought the knowledge to bring on a change in life and their community.

The founders were blessed with the mental capabilities to do things that other organizations would never dream to do.
God was and still is the focus of the change.
Like wolves the brothers shall cunningly take over and become once again the kings of earth. The brothers unlike any fraternal order or religion for the matter of arguments, combined aspects from different religions to create a order of the brotherhood that was sort of in the middle of reality and conscious.
From different religions it brought new aspect to intertwined among each other to make a new understanding that would change the attitude of a fallen but prosperous race and keep it that way.
From Buddism it uses the enlightenment method of the mind and soul.
From Taoism and Confucianism it uses the Ta Hsueh (pronounced Ta S-u-eh or the great learning) which makes the brotherhood what it truly is, not a fraternity not a religion but an understanding.

And the undying faith of the teaching of Christianity, for every sun rise in this world let another black son know that he is King. Due to the knowledge of the brotherhood in the time of the enlightenment's creation the brotherhood decided to break the knowledge down into four understandings and five rewards.
The brotherhood does not care about how much you know,
but of how much you can understand
The order is to represent a strong and prosperous man in life,
in exeption to your work or pleasure habits.
Brothers are to represent (Chun-tzu) a gentleman or superior man.
Because there is a time and place for everything you do.

To My Brothers (Part One)

Life Short and Sweet

**It's ironic that so many of us waste our life on bullshit.
So many of us die without accomplishing shit.
Why can't we realize that if we live a 100 years without doing anything in life we'll become a lost chapter in a eternal constant called time.
It is good to be remembered for doing something in life so when your gone you can continuously be responsible for influencing life.
Forever more letting people feel how you bonded to life.
See the unique thing about life is how you experience it,
it is never duplicated by anyone else on earth.
Every human body and mind that lives now,
lived before or will live soon will experience life differently.
So it's good to let others know how you feel.
Cause see time is a rolling beast that let's you come in and feel the wonderful sensations that reality has to give.
Then it comes back along and snatches you away and rolls on
until you are forgotten.
But if you influence the lives of generations to come then you defeat time by bonding with it to the point where your essence rolls on with it.**

Let me know, Tell me so?

When will we get together and know what together means?

When will we hold each other and know that we are brothers and sisters?

Please let me know.

Can you tell me so?

What happen to my past?

Where am I at?

Where will I go?

How long will the clouds blur my visions of what I see?

Please let me know.

Can you tell me so?

Expression Eight

Hold your head up high and reach to the Heavens.
Let no man tell you that you are lower or meek.
For in your own way you are different and that makes you special
and ask not why I hold my head the way I do.
For I don't see above or below you but from within and around you.

Table of Togetherness

I am the off-spring of the slaves,
I am the dream they made,
I am the price they paid,
I walk the street they paved,

I am petrified by souls of pain,
Love and hate to the table of togetherness is what I bring,
I am their life and their death,
I am their pain and their hapiness,

Their light grows in me so bright that you could not begin to conceive,
I am the ocean of hopes and dreams that they could not achieve

When will we realize an improvise,
Why can't we signify and unify,
We always try to simplify and deny,
To rise as one,

Rise as no one has ever risen before,

They bequeathed me with an arsenal of knowledge
and I must now bequeath it to the next generation,

Blessed with a history of greatness and grandeur not
to be repeated on earth,
I am a black man, I am a proud man,
I am a great man, I am a legendary man,

With a past behind me and future ahead,
I will fight to preserve it until the day I am dead,

So when I come to the table of togetherness
I bring with me a great contribution
of millions before me,
And a coming of contributions of millions for eternity.

Unify

Band your hands together
and lift your voice to the sky,
You are mighty, you are powerful,
and great until you die.
You grace this planet as a race
of many shades,
For you are of ones that were exploited
for things you made.
For so long you were in battle
against others,
Now you conflict against your sisters
and your brothers.
But things can get better.
We must get this might race to
come together.

**Cause the power of a nation is what the male
of this race holds,
While the all true woman is pure
as 24karat gold.
So let us bond together as tough
as the hide of a whale,
Cause becoming one is the
only way we can never fail.
We came a long way and our road
is still very far,
But to become what we want we
must find out who we are.
For we are of those that can
never be another,
So stand up you great color
UNIFY.**

To My Sisters (Part One)

Pain (My song to You)

You could never imagine how I felt about you,
If I could have snatched the stars from the sky I would have given them to you,
If I could have made the moon glow only for you at night I would have
I would have changed the course of a river if you'd have asked,
And yet through all the devotion I gave, you would not show me one grain of emotion,
I would have been anything you wanted me to be,
done anything you wanted me to do,
and you still would not show me that you would be there for me,
and when only one part of a relationship is giving and the other is only taking it hurts,
It hurts like having your soul stretched and broken,
or a million pound cylinder block slammed down on your chest over and over.

Relationships

I walk gracefully into the local place in my city where everyone is,
I see you so fly, so beautiful I have to have you,
Like the fox I approach, so swift I startled you,
We conversate and I aquire your name,
Within time we love each other but I still must be the mack of the year or my boys will call me soft,
When you really need me I'm not there cause I'm with her and you storm away,
I'm hurt but can't show it and that makes you madder,
She does the same to me after I believe I really need her,
my world is now crushed and I wish I had you,
I go find you crying and pleading that you come back but you don't,
Cause you feel you could never trust me again,
Because my image meant more to me than you at the time,
I have lost you and my whole world.

I'm sorry baby!

Trapped

In a unescapable cell locked away from you is my soul,
Your walk sets off torches in my heart, your talk sparked emotions that flood me with love,
But I can't have you cause I can't talk to you,
You are so beautiful, so strong willed,
From a distance is my love,
I know not if we could be together or if we can't cause I don't want to take that chance to ask you,
Together we could be but my heart hurts cause I can't ask you for to you I am shy,
To be trapped so far away that my words take years to be recieved,
Yet to be trapped so close I can feel your beautiful skin,
Puts a burden on my heart equal to the weight of a mountain,
As I fill with sorrow and cry tears long enogh to make small gray lakes of pain and love.

My Chestnut love affair

My hands ride through chestnut hair,

Streaking across a carmel candy colored body,

My inspirations are endless around you my dear chestnut love affair,

As vivid as flickering specs of light on a calm night,

Wild as a free spirit yet controlled as a mathmatical system,

Your smile is lovely,

Your eyes like two sexy knives cutting through my soul,

Your lips like two sweet strawberries touching my skin so soft,

My chestnut love affair.

Please

Let me make love to and all through your body,

Can I play with your soul,

Baby every touch is meant to make you surge with passion,

To put it blunt I want to tranquilize you in exstacy,

I need to feel the earth move at the first body quenching orgasm,

Can I, let me please come, come inside you till I can't come no more,

I live inside you so warm and sweet my lady please.

Tortured soul of love

**Why do you torture me with your magnificent ways,
Your sweet sounds of love the voices of exstacy,
You bury me alive with what you do yet I am still in
love with you,
You give me a friendly kiss on my cheek,
When I fien to exoticly move you,
You give me a nice hello,
When I yearn to make love to you,
To me you are insatiable,
To you I am a friend,
To me you are sheer electricity,
To you I am a but fallen leaves,
As touching as autumn,
Your beauty is as strong as an antient land of
lovely wanwood,
Yet you tantalize and take away and leave
me crying for your touch every
God given day.**

Love you for Me

My insatiable Angel, Sweet as sweetness can get,

I give my heart to you, Until I can give no more,

I propose a toast to you on every coast that bears your presence

You need affection and I need your being as enlightening as a beautiful song,

You make my heart glow as bright as the sun in the sky.

My Sista'

She walks with grace equal to angels,

Beautiful as a walk in the rays of the sun,

If you are her friend she can be as a ride on a quiet and exotic lake,

But if you are her enemy she can be as mean and deadly as a violent hurricane,

Yet she is my love, my calling and my heart,

She comes in many beautiful shades from a light skinned princess to a dark chocolate goddess.

Soft - n - Sweet

My tears flow from my eyes as oceans,

I see forever in the flash of one moment,

Feelings flutter through me like birds in the sky,

And I can't control it.

I am the one that sees you but can't hear for I
am lost in thought,

I am the one that knows you but can't
understand what makes you so beautiful,

Naturally fantastic,

Roots and essence is your keys to life,

Unlock the lock that opens the door to my heart,

For my door is the entrance to eternity.

Beautiful

I regret seeing you, because it could never compare to the
day I first layed eyes on you,
the mystique in your eyes,
the desire in your every move,
the richness of your soul is shown
through the darkness of your hair,
so illustrious,
there is no need to fear I'm here,
compassion and sensitivity it's here,
if you ever need to talk to me come here,
please be my shinning star my dear,
you are a gift that I feel unworthy of having,
you are a beauty that I fear to touch,
you send my soul to realms beyond the beyond,
I can see the colors of the rainbow in your eyes,
I can hear the songs of angels when you speak,
you are beautiful,
so sweet,
as lovely as a sun set in the caribbean sea,
quiet and peaceful as a long walk
through the China gardens,
you are an honor,
I kneel before you,
I kiss your feet,
Beautiful.

Tonight

Tonight our journey to exstacy will begin,
but Tonight first let me look and be possessed and obsessed
by what Heaven baked in your honey brown skin.

Tonight take off all your clothes,
for Tonight I want to play with your very soul.

Tonight I want to taste the sweetness of your juice,
Tonight I want you to let your mind loose.

Tonight the peak of you sexual drive is what I intend to hit,
Tonight I want to be your bitch.

Tonight my dear I'll do anything you say,
cause Tonight I want to love you in every way.

Tonight all I want to do is have you next to me,
Tonight all I want to do is here the sounds of pure exstacy.

Tonight may I please, beg of you to have a drink,
Tonight of what makes you a woman so soft, so intelligent, so magnificent, so powerful, so pink.

Tonight my love I want you to know,
Tonight I would be damned to let you go.

Moments of Forever

To electrify everything you touch is what you are meant for,

To be magnificent is what you are meant to be,

You are the most beautiful creation on the face of the world,

May I hold your hand forever and from forever to infinity,

You get me high as a narcotic when I am with you,

I am a fool for you unwrapping.

Sisters all the way round

I love ya thick, I love ya thin,
I love ya Down, I love ya round,

I love ya smile, An when ya wild,
I'm infatuated by your style,

I love ya best, Beautifully blessed,
Lay your love on my chest,

You are so sweet, I kneel at your feet,
Next to me please take your seat,

I adore your ways, All of my days,
In your mind may I stay.

Tribute to you the Black Woman

**To me,
You are equal to no one,
To love yo is my happiness,
To hold you is to have a soft brown angel in my arms,
To look at you is to see unmatched beauty,
A blossoming flower in early spring,
Heart as warm as a summer day,
Pure as the snow that falls in winter,
Your power can only be overseen by your beauty,
And your beauty only overseen by your power,
Your eyes like two exploding supernova's of passion,
Your skin soft as a summer breeze,
Hair flows from your head like a river from a stream,
Your attitude is your strength, your heart, and your will,
You are in class by yourself,
You let loose your anger through an exotic fullfillment of passion and lust,**

------> If you please ----->

Thank you.........

Thou if I could take the sun and place it in your soft warm hands I would,
And if I could take the moon and put it in your sweet brown eyes I would,
If I controlled the wind I would blow all your troubles away,
If I possessed the seven seas I would drown you in exstacy,
Oh how I wish to have one true black woman as you,
To stand at my side I will promise to cherish and adore you forever,
So I willingly kneel to your humble presents as you make the world glow,
When you walk within the heavenly blue sky,
And it is my honor to look at you through my hazel eyes,
And may I say that I am beyond joy to have had the blessing to touch you with my God given flesh,
Because you are my heart, my soul, my power, and my mind and I love you Black Woman.

To the 1 you Love

To my Scorpio

And to you that chocolate beautiful that made my heart pump at a million miles a minute, I want you.

In the dreams of all my days I saw you, and the moment my heart jumped in overdrive for you was sweeter than all those dreams put together.

Now I can see us so vividly in a candlelite room talking endlessly until the morning sun rises and pours its golden glow all over us.

Must I bathe you in rose pedals and lilacs, rub your body in warm oils and get blowed with you all night long, lick you from your head to the bottom of your feet to prove to you that I want you and I need you.

Because if thats the case then everyday I'll do my best to provide that for you.

Or must I set you on a pedistal high in the sky where the world would have to say damn there sits his queen as beautiful as a senset burning in the western sky.

Because I will if you let me.

I want to love you with all that I am.

Loving you (from Afar)

Blessed with a touch of honey
beautiful beyond compare,

I would cherish everyday spent with you,

Love is what I am,

Magnificent is what you are,

You are my star that shines upon me from the Heavens,

You are as bright as the sun, and majestic as the moon,

You are what I live for.

My Incantation to Brown Sugar

Every characteristic is blessed by Heaven,
You bring enrapturing joy to those that come near you,
Optimistic in a sense your beauty is infinite,
Sweet as honey is your soul you are the true 24karat Woman,
And this is my Incantation to you Brown Sugar.

Feel You, See You, Hear You

Tender is what I feel when I kiss your lips,
Soft is what I feel when I hold your hand,
Sensual is what I see when I look in your eyes,
Grace is what I see in your walk,
Breathtaking is what I hear when you speak,
And I love it.

If you Were, I would Be

If you were a shepard, I would be your sheep.

If you were a Navy, I would be your most powerful fleet.

You are the sun to me that shines so bright,

You are the dreams that I hold so tight through the night.

If you were cold, I would be the heat that you seek.

If you were sad, I would be the tears that you weep.

I want to be as close to you as the perfume you wear on your flesh,

I want to support you like the bra you wear on your breast.

If you were a clock, I would be the bell that makes you ring.

If you were a singer, I would be the inspiration that makes you sing.

If you were a piano, I would be the sweet interlude that you play.

If you were a week, I would be your everyday.

You are the emotions that dwell in my heart,

You are the seam that keeps my soul from falling apart.

Quietstorm

You strolled into my life like a wander,

You implanted yourself in me like a weeping willow on a shore,

You were the passing ship that I saw daily but was scared to board,

And now you are the glowing quest I can never more ignore,

I play with the stars as I shift them to give them a reflection of you,

For how can they shine so bright in the sky if they do not shine for you,

You are that golden meadow that I once wanted to run through,

A fragrance created by fire and cooled by desire.

For how can a pearl be called a jewel if it does not retain a image of you,

I have found my quietstorm in that instance of forever,

Because around the inside of this quietstorm so dark shhh! can you hear the rain pouring to the ground like words from a mouth,

But I do not fear the dark because in the eye of this quietstorm I'm alright
for with me in the eye of the storm you stand next to me.

Au'vra twa Dis'tau Don'tai
(Peace may we bring us closer together)

You Are, You Are

As beautiful as untouched sands on a virgin shore
You Are, You Are

As bright as a comet strieking through a star filled sky
You Are, You Are

As soft as silk on a summer night blown against my skin
You Are, You Are

As tender as a flower in the spring freshly grown
You Are, You Are

As strong as thunder pounding into my imagination on a stormy spring night
You Are, You Are

As gentle as the atmosphere on a carol filled christmas eve
You Are, You Are

The one that I love more than anything on earth
You Are, You Are

You Are, You Are
(The Beautiful Rewrite)

Micheal Angelo couldn't begin to create a masterpiece as you
You Are, You Are
A living poem so pure so true
You Are, You Are
As luxurious as the rainbow in the sky
You Are, You Are
A love song that gets better as the day goes by
You Are, You Are
A novel of a thousand pages couldn't begin to see
You Are, You Are
The thousand beautiful things you would mean to me
You Are, You Are
I look, I see, I touch, I feel
You Are, You Are
And soon you shall see that this will be real
You Are, You Are

Expression Seventeen

The stars that fell from the sky gently placed
themselves in the center of my eye,
And flickered until they sparked a flame within me for you,
My soul hollers out through my flesh
I'll give you all that I am and not a damn thing less,
I embrace you like a hungry man does food,
I wrap myself up in you like a baby in a womb,
I let a candle burn for you all night your so tight,
seduce me with your love until the hour of light,
You intoxicate me like a drug
I'm so high then you leave me like a child in bed
where I lie,
Then the tears roll tenderly across
my cheek and fall into a endless puddle beneath my feet,
A grown man yet why do I cry laying in
loneliness and waiting to die.

A Letter to my Love

Their is something I want to tell you,
So I'm writing you this letter, to tell you what
it is,
My life is an infinite void unfullfilled beggin'
and hoping to be filled so I will not destroy myself,

This is how I feel,

Sometimes I walk out in my backyard and wish that
I could see your face in the stars,
So I just stare and gaze at the night sky cause
I know,
that is where you are,
In a beautiful cluster of splendor,
And as tears fall and burst into a ocean
of dreams,

I just want to look at you and hold your hands
you are so beautiful,
Sometimes I want to call the radio station and
dedicated every love song to you,

I can only hope that I am everything you want me
to be,
Cause I am real, I am sincere, I am love beyond
all you can see,
I am love to the fullest extent,
From earth to every realm in imagination I am love,
And I will be whatever you want me to be,
I listen to the wind blow the leaves in the trees
and they tell me a story of you,

And I listen to the raindrops fall from the sky
to the ground and they also tell me a story,

And I love you.

I Love you Enough

**I love you enough...
That to just know your name I would travel
distances beyond that of reality.
All the way into cosmic fantasies,
And worlds of illusions that send me into paradise,**

**And I love you enough...
That to win your heart I would fight
Heaven and Hell and all the men on earth,
And not lose.
I would tackle the essence of life.
And slam the inevitables of death.**

**I love you enough...
That to keep you I would tell you sweet
beautiful words in motions of water,
continuously.**

**Like if a poet is only as good as his inspiration,
then surely you are the inspiration of Juliet
in the mind of Shakesphere.**

**And I love you enough...
That if you wanted to be free,
I would release you into this
land of dreams and contemptments.
Honored truths and evil damnations.**

**Touch me like a autumn gathering of colored trees.
Your beautiful smile embraces
me like a mother does a child.
I love you enough...
To love you.**

**And I love you enough...
That I would stimulate you mentally and physically in every way.
I would lick your soul like honey from my hands.
Make you so weak that you could not stand.**

**I love you enough...
To love you.**

You are Mine

As God created this world,
I shall create love in your heart for me,

As music has a beat,
As humans have two feet,

I will have you,

The way exstacy goes to sex,
The way a hooker goes to the next,

You will be mine,

I shall wash your feet,
I shall taste you so sweet,

You shall be the concern of the night,
You shall hold me close and very tight,

I scream your name, you are the best,
As I lick the sweat dripping from your flesh,

You are mine,

As Ice comes from the cold,
And greed comes from gold,

As illustrious as the sparkle of jewels,
You will be mine.

How I feel about You

When I am asked about you,
I say,
The fire within me for you is so
hot that I could burn the world,
I worship you like a queen and embrace you like a little girl,
Tears shred my face at the thought of losing you,
You set my world right with the things you do,
You are a happiness I sometimes feel unworthy to bare,
And like the ending of a fairy tale,
ever after is the world we share,
When I look at you I dive deep into your eyes,
And I play with your soul everytime you let me come inside,
To be with you is my only request,
In this life I place my head on your
breast till the moment of my death,
To make you happy is all I see,
You smile is my smile and that's the way it should be,
In the moon you shimmer, In the sun you glare,
If Heaven is what you want hold my hand I'll take you there,
Come with me there is no pain where I go,
I love you now and then and forever more,
That's what I think about when asked of you.

My Wife, My Friend

**And in my world I wonder,
you queen born from a black child,
How could you have been raised
into the woman I like,
A woman I've grown to
love, cherish and adore,
My momma raised me to a man and I grew into a human
being when I join my soul with you,
Your what I want, You what I want,
From your head to your feet,
your heart and your eyes,
To your soul, to your kiss,
and the tenderness between your thighs,
Na' baby, I hope that you believe in me deep down in your
heart, I pray and I—I plead love me forever more,
Take me on a ride on a blanket of stars
on an eternal shore,**

Let's make people envy the love we have
so beautiful, so enchanting so free,
So passionate, so glamorous,
so wonderful to me,
Without a thought you are the
right hand of my life,
While God oversees us and
I'm glad that your my wife,
Hold me, squeeze me, taste me,
I want to be your favorite wine,
Think about me constantly I want to
be the dreams in your mind,
Girl your the flower I
love to hold,
The little bunny I protect from
the cold,
Don't you cry their is no
need to fear,
I'm comin' when you need just
call and I'll be there.

Lived my Life with You

**My soul at magnificent speeds races across this world,
to see everything
I wanted to see,
Showed me everything I ever wanted to know,
I knew it was over a while ago,
I just couldn't tell you so,
I couldn't find a way in my heart to let
you know that I had to go,
But baby through all that shit that I did
in my life I'm glad that I lived my life with you,
Now I understand looking down upon you
as you cry over me, exactly what you meant to me,
Your touch was so wonderful it made me feel so good,
your smile every morning as bright as the sun,
When we argued, when we fought,
cried and made up in one night,
It made living worth wild,**

And I'm glad I lived my life with you,
I shared the fears that I keep locked
down within me with you,
my secret that very few could know,
With you I leave my essence and what I stood for,
like the Holy Ghost in the form of a dove
let my love descend down upon you and ease your mind,
You meant the world to me and
I pray to see you once again in forever,
Ya know I never really thought about death
until she came and stole my breath,
viciously tearing my soul from my flesh,
And I told her I'm glad I lived my life with you,
I told her to remember you when she came for you in the future,
And to let you go beautifully and peacfully into paradise,
For you make me become a provider,
a husband and a man to please you,
and I thank you.

I am truly glad I lived my life with you.

A Garden, A Terrace, Then You
(The Epilogue)

Your wonderful smile is my anthem,
As I rise in the morning mist,
The smell of fresh tender baby leave wet from shimmering grey waterfalls intoxicates my mind as your image dances on the retna of my eyes,
The purity of the morning seems to make an angelic glow around you as you stare at me in the young sun,
The liquid diamonds shine so radiantly like sprinkles across the earth while you glare like carmel gold wrapping in a sheet of soft white,
Your voice so soft over the beautiful singing of birds and the sound of a metropolis awakening tantalize me in ways you could not believe,
I walk out on the grass bare to the sensation the tingling cool spring wetness is astounding to my soul, I kneel and pluck a flower from the ground so sensual damp and lovely,
The color so deep and rich I hold it close to my nose and with a deep breath I inhail the sweet nectar of natures finest scent,
I looked up at the terrace and see you looking passionately at me,
I never thought on that first day I saw your face in the window of that terrace,
Although I so vividly dreamed that I would be way down in the wells of your essence so physically, so mentally, so spiritually,
And I loved every blessed moment that I lived in the yard of your sexuality and emotions.
See You
In Eternity

This Night with You

Oh let my love wrap you like a cool mist on a hot summers day,
Bringing you a uncontrollable relief,
Your breast like two soft spheres of delight,
invites me across the room to where you are,
to what you are,
The heat has made a lite gloss of perspiration across your flesh,
I lick it from your hands, your arms, your shoulders, your neck,
I take you in my arms strong yet tender and sweet,
Are you fine?
You naturally fit in my world,
As if God designed us to be,
Your scent I want to bottle and spray on me when we're apart,
Wonderfully we lay in bed,
and roll into our own world so exquisitely,
I suck at you,
You suck at me,
I kiss your toes,
lick your legs,
then take soft bites across your beautiful ass,
Your beautiful brown ass,
I firmly rub my hands up and down your back,
Do you like that?
And how about this thumb up the soft of your back?
I roll you over and lick your stomach then began to ravish your breasts,
putting more soft bites on your nipples and neck,

You voice like a tender siren of love,
calls me to your lips,
We kiss as I stare deeply in your eyes,
I love eyes,
And I really love your eyes,
The way their wanting me,
You roll me over,
And baby,
Oh! my goodness,
Began putting passionate kisses all over my chest,
Then you go down to my hardness,
No hands,
And attack me till my bottom lip trembles with joy,
Then I take you and lay you on your back,
Spreading your legs and sinking my tongue
deep in your brown and pink folds,
And I suck on you till you began to shake,
and your screams echo through the valley's of my mind,
I rise and stare at you,
the scent of sex is everywhere,
And I know you wanting to fill
me all inside your needing frame,

I enter your dark and sensuous depths,
And shake at the feeling of your wondrous constriction,
Girl fit yourself around me,
You could never imagine how this feeling astounds me,
I pound, and I pound,
then I glide so softly,
Then I pound, and I pound, and I pound,
Then I stop,
and I glide so softly,
Then I pound, and I pound, and I pound, and I pound,
Then I stop
and I glide so softly,
Then I pound,
And I pound till you scream in ecstasy,
And I explode like that great day if independence,
Filling the canal inside you with the sweetness of my life,
We rest next to each other,
touching and talking,
Till we do it again, and again, and again,
then we fall asleep,
in a bundle of cover and sheets,
And when the sun rises and lays it's warm hands on your eyes,
I awake and look at you as you sleep,
I kiss your cheek and your forehead,
I love you so,
Every morning I arise to your face is like a blossoming flower,
So beautiful as it arrives in spring,
I am so glad your mine.

Oh My! Oh My!

When I met you young pretty
and the joy of life in your eyes,
I fell in love with you.
I've watched you grow over the
years into the seasoned and most
elegant woman that I have here,
today.
Your smile as beautiful as the
thoughts of another day of my life,
I love you.
Your eyes two pools of deep rich jewels
looking into my soul so wonderful.
Your voice a glorious beckon to my ears
like the voice of a angel calling
me home so Heavenly.

To the Father of Creation
and his vision of Life
(Part One)

God's Touch

As beautiful as the fire colored clouds of sunset,
Flowing in a endless sky like liquid sheets of satin,
God's touch electrifies your soul,
As luscious as the water of a sea,
Bonding into a mass captivating blue entity,
God's touch electrifies your heart,
As stimulating as a green pasture,
Waving at the sky like a lavishing green cloth of silk,
God's touch electrifies your mind,
And as mighty as a giant grey mountain,
Standing unchallenged in a blue masterpiece of a skyline,
God's touch electrifies your life.

For Forgiveness Peace

**The seeds of Heaven bless us all,
But the roots of evil will make us fall,
For man all the time can never follow
the true instruction,
On his road of learning and road of destruction,
In life he went through adultery, racism, prostitution,
enslavery, hatred, false education, and still he lives on,
But only through death is how he will truly get along,
For as long as man pumps hatred and pain through his veins,
God will let the great blue sky rain,
Cause the raindrops are the angels tears as they cry upon you
So don't call Heaven when bad things
happen cause you brought it upon yourself,
So when the sheep are picked from the earth like the fruit of a tre
The wolves will run ravaging, for death is what they see,
They will run and run until they can run no more,
Then fall to their knees and beg in the eyes of the Almighty Lord.**

Expression Four

**If God is alpha and omega,
If he is big and small,
If he is all and everlasting,
If he is great and all knowing,
If he is forever and almighty,
Then who are we to say who is,
Righteous or who are sinners,
When we can never be as perfect,
As he, the great infinite,
We are mere fragments in his cosmic puzzle,
Yet we claim to be superior,
When we cannot cause the earth to shake and split open,
And we cannot cause the water to rise up against,
The land as hurricanes,
Or make the wind turn into a
mighty monolith of power,
As a tornado,
But we can be swept and destroyed
by these great magnificent,
Reap what you sow,
Sow what you reap,
But remember in and on his chess
board you are a very small piece.**

Expression Ten

God o' ye that liveth,
God o' ye that giveth,
God o' ye that eases us when we bleed,
God o' ye that provides
right on time when we need,
I love you.

Expression Fourteen

I fear my great creative field will die,
Music is tome the greatest God/man made creation ever formed
Voices blessed by God and music by man,
A magnificent collaboration not to be duplicated ever again,
The only creation that needs both God and man to do,
Yet greed is now destroying that bond,
I give thanks to those who keeps creativity first,
For I hope I die before the devil destroys my one true passion.

The Creator

I love creating more than I love myself but not as
much as I love the Father of all creators,
I love making music more than I love myself
but not as much as the Heavenly Father,
I love art more than I love myself but not
as much as the Master of Heaven,
I love writting more than I love myself but not
as much as my omnipotent Lord of Lords,
For he gives me my drive and creative passion,
For His is Almighty,
GOD.

If the Bible could speak

**Is it so astonishing physically ain't no stoppin' me,
To those who thought they were toppin' me ended so shockingly
I've stood strong, disciples raised up tall,
While others raised themselves to conqueor then fall,
First it was given to you, yet you did not understand,
Then it was taught and you rejected the form of man,
Now you know and choose to ignore,
Living in your own understanding casting me away like sores,
Anything you need and want I have to give,
Yet you dance in darkness of how you choose to live,
As the wind your mind's change and blow so frequently,
And when the beast comes you realize you need me,
Read and learn, understand and apply,
Live your life for me, and you I will magnify.**

The First Book of Shiyon and The Celestial Psalms of I BE

The First Book of Shiyon
Verse One: Laws of the Song

And the Lord spoke unto Shawn
and said you are my song Alpha,
you are my song Omega,
So when you write,
it will be not what you doeth
but how you doeth it,
that will make you great,
And not what you see but how you
seeth it that will make you great,
Unto your songs make beauty unto
me in order to make beauty unto you,
Make thou songs of the heart and soul,
not the mind for the Lord your God commands it,
Make true your visions of life,
and prosperity shall be complete unto you,
Let skies of blue and grey and white enhance
your sight of which you seeth,
Let leaves of light green, red,
yellow, and orange fill your mind and thoughts,
Let the sun that I giveth bless the brightness of your heart,
Be one with my beauty that I give so that you can be one with thyself,
Let the motion of my Heaven caress thee and guard thee at all times,
Write love as strong as the Lord,
I give unto you and thou shall be great for I am the Lord your God,
Listen to these words of me and you shall make people love,
Write in the season of leaveth leaves and you shall
create harmony of the Heaven and of your soul.

The First Book of Shiyon
Verse Two: Laws of the Sun

**And the Lord spoke unto Shawn in his thoughts,
Unto the sun that I give unto you everyday
praise me for I am your God,
Let my warm rays of gold bles
your skin that I giveth,
Thou Shawn inform them that they
can never have the sun forever,
So enjoy the sun while thee have it,
You are to praise me your God everyday
for giving you the privilege to see the sun,
Thou shall see gold in the skies of blue and white,
Thou shall walk in the praire and stop for seven hours,
on the seventh day of the seventh month,
in the seventh year and kneel to
praise me in thought,
But if thou worship the sun more than I,
you God,
then let my anger be kindled upon thy people,**

The First Book of Shiyon
Verse Three: Rains of Heaven

Heavens thoughts once again poured into the
thoughts of Shawn and said:
This is the meaning of the rains of Heaven,
A rain shower is just a washer of uncleaness,
Heavy showers washes away evil,
Storms are made when you,
they people have kindled the anger of thy
Lord and when they people have forgotten that
I am the Almighty Lord of Lords, my anger is
kindled to the heat of the core of Earth,
And I unleash tornadoes, hurricanes,
earthquakes, typhoons,
and tidal waves.

The First Book of Shiyon
Verse Four

**Let your soul be bound by goodness and joy,
Let your eyes show the greatness of my power,
Let your body be wrapped in my love,
For only I can give you everlasting,
Show the green pastures that yield your
fruit to those that may not see,
Give heart from deep within you too,
those who otherwise may not feel,
Give the light of joy from your
being to those that may not hear,
And I the Lord will bless you,
For I am Almighty the gift giver and gift taker,
For I give you everything from life,
to the smallest crumbs you eat and you
shall put no one, nothing and no place before me,
Praise thee the Almighty.**

The Celestial Psalms of I BE
The Celestial Prayer

Mercy! I am glad you have that
for me. It is a blessing to know that you
understand my iniquities and give me the opportunity
to repent in my wrongs to your wonderful and glorious
right.
Pleasures! I know that's what life is all about in
your presence when you return on that great and awesome
day. To gather those who believe in you and know that your
love is true.
Graciously! Take me by the soul and
lead me to your table and feed me with your bread
and enhance my senses with the sweetness of your mind
like aged wine.
Tenderly! Hold me in your arms and rub my head
like a baby on your shoulder. Like a spoiled child
I cry when you put me down, keep me in your love.
I love you!

The Flesh, The Soul

The Celestial Psalms of I BE

The Flesh
Majesty with a Savior and Lord like you
who can cry,
why would we cry,
who could know the meaning,
Father with a All Mighty everlasting love as you
who can die,
why would we die,
who could know the meaning,
King with a unmatched forgiveness as you
who would feel pain,
why would we feel pain,
who could know the meaning,
God my wonderful Emperor of light,
with fair and righteous judgement
who can lie,
why would we lie,
who could know the meaning,
The Soul
Master with a gift giver as giving as you
why do we hurt,
why do we know the meaning,
My host of paradise who created all that I see and feel
O' why do we lust of the flesh
why do we know the meaning.

Fortress of my Heart

The Celestial Psalms of I BE

Favorfully I shine in the eyes of my
Omnipresent let you
Righteousness glow in my
Tainted and
Revelry filled flesh
Express your deep
Satisfaction in the way I try my best to stop
Sinful thoughts

It's not easy to hold
Off these
Feeling that

Manifest in my body and make me
Yearn for more

But
Heaven your
Eternity is
Ascending slowly down to be
Rightfully with me and I want to live within it truly and
Totally.

Forgive Me

The Celestial Psalms of I BE

O' my sorrow is full to
the top of my mind,
Father I have sinned in the
night and I know you saw it
like broad day light,
What can I do my flesh
has got the best of me,
tonight,
I have to regain my spirit
please have faith in me, forgive
me my Father, I do love
you, but in the heat of
passion I looked away from
your word that is so good
and so right,
Help me Father O' please in your
Christ Jesus I cry to the
top of my lungs forgive me,
It's not easy to battle
temptation in the physical
form,
I'm new and still lukewarm,
Refill me with your word
so I can build anew,
Don't throw me away help me to try again.

I hope I'm Ready
The Celestial Psalms of I BE

Oh Father, Father, Father, Father, Father,
I love you,
I love you and all your ways,
I hope you see,
What you do to me,
And when you call me home,

I hope I'm ready,
I hope I'm ready,
I hope I'm prepared,
I hope I'm prepared,
I hope your happy,
With what you see,
I hope your happy,
When you look at me,

Oh Father, Father, Father, Father, Father,
I'm sorry,
I'm sorry for the wrong I have done,
Take me softly in your arms,
Fly me gently cross the sky,
And when you call me home,

I hope I'm ready,
I hope I'm prepared.

Reflections in the Future (Looking Back)
The Celestial Psalms of I BE

"And I say to you beast of this world, I shall not call you king of my life or keeper of my soul. I will not take your mark, I will not call you lord most high. See if those who follow you and take your mark willingly could open their eyes and see just how horrible you really are then your power would be meaningless."

"I spit on your power and I laugh at your authority, you are nothing to me. Fuck what I have done in my life, from this moment on I stand to serve GOD the True and All-Mighty. Not that I did not serve him before, but now in full strength I resist you. I have never forgotten him through my course in life but I also have not done all that he has commanded of us in this body. And in the body of his wonderful son Jesus Christ my ultimate preacher and shepard."

"But you who exalt yourself on earth over his glorious name and peace I can only feel sorrow for you. For you know there is no way you can stop the One untouched by your evil and wicked ways. I know the actions you take against me proves that you are a terrible being driven by your own sheer desires. But I would rather please you with my dead blood spilled across this earth, than to please you on my knees hailing your name."

"Now before your wicked congregation I stand bloody and drained of all that I am. For your amusement I have been beaten, punished, and put down like a animal. But my Father, you believe me, will come and give me a breeze through the heat you have inflicted on me. He will run the cool waters of Heaven down apon my scorched flesh. You and your ways mean nothing to me, when I know that I am meant to go to another place. A place of splender and elegance especially prepared for me."

Now I don't know if I have been good enough to go to Heaven or bad enough for Hell, but I do know I will not worship you. So I proudly except death for the sake of my True Father in Heaven for only through him shall I live forever. I have let my body fall victim to many temptations on this earth, but I refuse to let my soul bow to you and your false Godlihood."

"It upsets you I know, just the emotion I was looking for. I watch as your face swells with hatred for me and I laugh. Ha! You worthless and spiteful being you, I piss on your honor. I feel my stomach turns at the sight of you. Throw all of my iniquities in my face all you want beast, I shall feel no shame for what I have done, for I did it in clear conscious. Yes! To my Father in Heaven I am sorry for failing victim to my sinful ways, not

because of shame but because I know it made you upset at the sight of my actions.

Lord in Heaven Almighty I have sinned many times some known, some unknown but I will not live in a world governed by this creature."

"I have pleased myself with the pleasures of this world many days, but I have not tried to hurt anyone in my life on purpose, and to anyone that I have hurt in anyway in my life I am sorry. If you forgive me or not is truly up to you, I did my part with GOD as my witness. If you had not come beast my life probably would have went on for many years, for I stood firm at the commandment of honoring my Mother and Father, eventhough I was with my Mother the majority of my life."

"See it took me many years to realize that life is a test of many different series of questions. Each day a different series of questions needing a different series of answers, and I know I decided on a lot of fucked up answers in my life. I stand here at the end of my life asking myself the ultimate question. Why? Why didn't I do right when I should have? Why didn't I do right when I could have? Why didn't I do right when it was downright necessary? And I could go on and on."

"You know beast I can not figure out why we as human beings cannot find a way to love one another the way we love the desires we lust after. I mean we as human beings love sex, drugs, and claim to love GOD more than we love one another. I use to smoke weed all day or trick with cheap freaks for money, money I could have used to help someone in need, but instead I enjoyed myself for pleasure in a controlled moment in time when I could have helped someone for a long time in life."

"I let your demons of this world tell me I was better than someone else cause I wore expensive clothes and gym shoes and they wore cheaper shit. How nieve can a mutha fucka' be. I ain't nothing but another person that's going to die if I'm rich or poor."

"How many hearts have I broken in my lifetime? So many lies, I love you! Powerful words that makes women believe you so deeply, especially when they are young and just beginning to experience life. To brothers who dealing with my ex-partners and going through some shit I'm sorry. It was the bullshit in me that did it. It's funny that we as men have two true facts that make us do what we do, and if we could pass these two facts we would be all right.

1) We want to love every woman we see.

2) We need to be loved by that one true woman.

And what I'm saying is we want to have sex with every woman we see, but we need to have that one we can run to in need."

"And you know I have understood the reason why we sin. It is because our body knows it's going to die so it wants to feel and do all the desires it's

capable of because it knows it's going to die. Your body has a mind of it's own and it is terribly jealous and spiteful of your soul. It knows that the soul lives forever and it wants it to die in the second death the same way it has to die in the first death. That is why GOD says think with your soul so that you can think about forever. Cause your body only thinks of the right now and does all you can do for you. Think about it, you a ride across town in the middle of the night to have sex, or ride around all day looking for a hit of whatever you smoke, but won't get up on Sunday morning and go to church or read a bible, probably in a room in your house."

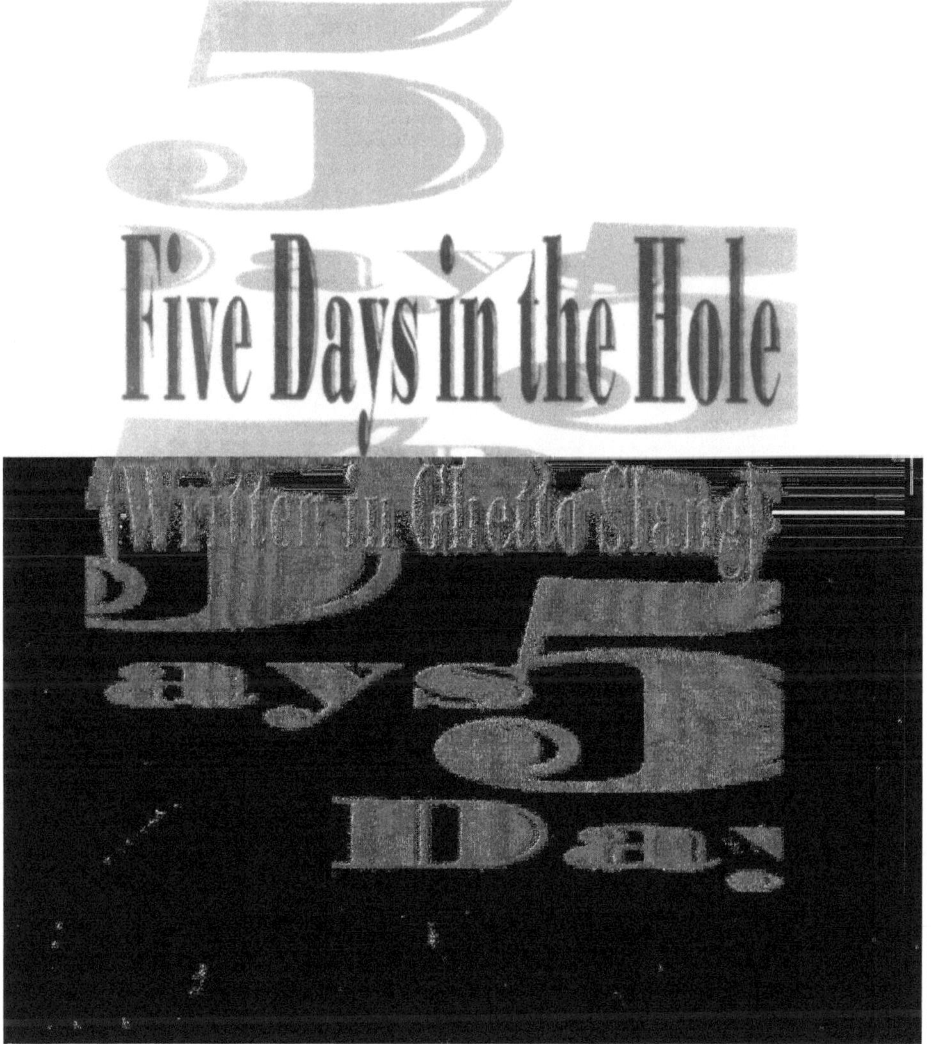
Five Days in the Hole
(Written in Ghetto Slang)

Day One

Nigga what! I use to know when it was time to get up in the mornin'. My man down stairs Javon would be on the porch every mornin' at 7:20a.m. on the nose smokin' a blunt. Me— shid, I knew that I had to be up and out the door by 8:15a.m. to catch the 8:24a.m. Van Dyke. It always worked out fine cause I didn't have to be at school until second hour and I had to smoke a bag before I got there. I would be blowed by the time I got to school, cause I would get off two blocks up and walk the rest of the way blowin' it.

Up in class high than a bitch, and really not givin' a fuck cause it was Geometry and I don't like math at all. My sister Tamika had Trig' second hour so I would try my best not to let her see me cause she would have told momma so mutha' fuckin' quick it wouldn't have been funny, but then I found out my sister was fuckin' and boy did that turn the tides quick. I love her fo-real tho', she a run a nigga pockets quick.

"Marcel! Marcel!"

"Ay what up doe?"

"You ain't hear me callin' you?"

"Yeah,— yeah what's goin' down?"

"Where the fuck was you at last night?"

"When?"

"When I called you and your sister said you was gone."

"What time?"

"Around nine, nine-thirty."

"I was at home, my sister just didn't want to get off the phone."

"Mmmmm Hmmmm"

"She just be sayin' that shit cause she don't want to get off the phone."

"Yeah whatever."

"For real."

"Okay then— fuck it."

"Fuck what."

"Fuck it, I'll just see you in lunch hour."

"Yeah, whatever."

"Mmmmm Hmmmm! Bye."

"Alright."

Her ass use to be flippin' all the time, I don't know why I was dealin' wit her shit, but she did have a fat ass. Damn she had a fat ass, and her mutha' fuckin' eyes would be lookin' so good when she was mad.

Hell yeah! I use to be thinkin' when third hour came around, when me and my nigga fo-life would be in class together fuckin' round and chillin'. Cornell, me and that nigga had been dogs since the third grade. Me and Corn as his nigga's call him, been through so much shit I couldn't begin to explain. My first blunt, my first time I fucked a female, and the first time I skipped school, shid I skipped over his house.

I remember when we use to hook up in art class and go to Corn's cousin Levell's house to watch the NCAA Tournament. Boy— do I remember that. Stoppin' at the store and givin' a crackhead or a drunk mu'fucka' some change to go in and buy us some forties galore. Be up in Corn's cousin's crib drunk than a bitch blowin' green's like a mutha' fuck.

"Ay yo Corn, what up doe?"

"Shit my nigga, nothin' at all."

"Where da' bitches at?"

"Only you know baby boy, cause I can't find one."

"Shid nigga you da' man."

"Whatever nigga, but fo-real. What's goin' down?"

"Nothin' my dog."

"My nigga guess what?"

"What up?"

"Sharell called me last night, and man it's on."

"Fo-real."

"Fo-real, and I mean fo-real."

"Henderson, Roberts!"

Mrs. Patton, she was our art teacher, my nigga she didn't bullshit, I'm tellin' you. She always wanted a nigga to make fake ass brass jewelry. I mean fo-real guy did she really expect a mu-fucka' to wear that shit. Not me, ain't no mutha' fuckin' way. Seein' nigga's wit real gold chains and braclets, and female's all ringed up, how was you gonna bang wit that. She was easy to manipulate, so easy that it became an obsession just to fuck wit her.

"Yes Mrs. Patton."

"Stop your talking, and listen at today's assignment."

"Yo, my nigga I'm a holla' at you in lunch."

"Fa-sho."

Corn had lunch fifth hour but like the whole click, we had I.D.'s for every hour of the day. Shid from third hour to sixth hour we would skip in the lunchroom, straight foolin'. Some days we would sit there every lunch hour, but most of the time we would rotate hours.

Mr. Westbrook was the lunch aide in fourth hour lunch, and he didn't bullshit. He was mean as hell and it was hard as fuck to sneak up in lunch when he was at the door, but we had learned how to get in though. All we had to do was start a diversion, a fakeass arguement or somethin' to set it

off. Mr. Westbrook wasn't gonna kick nobody out, he was just gonna leave the door and start droppin' all that so-called muslim knowledge on a mufucka'. That's when a nigga would slip right in and be chillin'. See we all knew that Mr. Westbrook was just gonna kick it to you like you was some kind of lost soul who didn't know how to be unified.

Once up in that bitch we would start clownin'. Fuckin' wit them lil' hoes, like what nigga what, but see I couldn't fuck around to long cause my girl would have been ready to start trippin' and I ain't want to have to cuss her ass out. I know she use to be watching me and shit thinkin', I was cheatin' on her. She was so jealous, somehow she didn't realize I was only with her. Sometimes I would wonder how she would feel if she found out that I had been with five girls sexually before I met her, and to this day she still dosen't know.

Her name Roshawn and I knew since the ninth grade, she was the first girl from my school that I had ever got involved with. See I'm the type of mutha' fucks' that liked to flirt and spit game, and you know how it is when your girl goes to the same school as you. No rest, but see— me and Roshawn, we had one beautiful thing in common, we loved to fuck. I couldn't count how many times we skipped school over my house and just banged. Damn that shit use to be good than a mutha' fuck, she use to moan alot, and she called a nigga name out so loud and talked so freaky.

"Fuck me Marcell Fuck me, oh-oh! It's yo' pussy, It's yo' pussy daddy."

Oh! I usc to love to hear that shit.

Her damn attitude could change as quick as a damn commercial. I mean cool one minute then mean as hell the next. She always a have to apologize after she blow up with all that bullshit. I knew why she did it, she was so damn insecure from all them other soft ass nigga's she had been dealin' with. So she thought that I was gonna treat her the same way. My boy Corn use to say that me and Roshawn was gonna be together forever because only I could deal with her shit. In a way that nigga was right cause she still with me to this day.

"Marcel."

"Ay what's up ba'."

"I'm sorry about earlier, my mind was goin' through some shit."

"It's alright girl— come here and gimme' mine."

I love to think about how soft that ass felt—, boy when I use to hugg her and cuff it."

"You a mutha' fuckin' freak."

"Hell yeah, when it comes to you girl."

"Tell me you love me?"

"Shid, you know I do."

"Then tell me?"

"I love you Roshawn."

"And I love you to."

I don't know maybe it was like I said, she was insecure or maybe she just liked hearing the shit. Oh— but I love her and all her ways to this day. She would always sit next to me holdin' my hand and layin' her head on my shoulder. I would feed her my lunch cause she would front like she wasn't hungry until I sat down with some food. On the real I liked being with her cause she let me just chill most of the time when I was with her. I found out though, how I don't know, that she liked to make me mad just so she could make up with me. Shit that she still do now in some of the letters I've got. I guess some things ain't gonna never change. I never really wanted to tell her that me and Corn was sellin' weed for Javon the nigga downstairs from me. I didn't know how she would react. I knew she was gonna figure it out one day, but until then I was gonna do my thang.

I remember my uncle use to tell me, Lil' nigga— bitches are always gonna be. They a love you if you paid, ridin' yo' dick, and they a love you if you broke if you make them take the dick. What you need to know is, fuck what you wear, fuck what you got, nigga— kick game. Make a bitch believe what you want her to believe. Cause ya' conversation is ya' key to a bitch. He would always make sure ya' ass was listenin'. Game a bitch up out her clothes, lil' nigga, fo-real. See make sure that you git that ass and when you get it, stomp the pussy through the floor. Eat the pussy, lick the ass, suck on the toes all that shit and he wasn't playin'. Don't do every hoe, he would say, cause all hoes wasn't ready for dat kinda' shit. Ugly nasty lookin' hoes, fuck dat, only fly lil' bitches.

I never really thought about that shit and when he would be tellin' me I would be thinkin' he was crazy. Eat the pussy, lick the ass damn is he sick, but he kept his hands on bad ass bitches.

He use to tell a nigga that, boy you don't want to get a B.D.R., and I use to wonder what that was. It was a Bad Dick Report and my uncle never ever wanted to hear a bitch say no shit like that about him or any nigga in his family, he was wild like that.

Now on the real, I didn't think about that shit until I met Roshawn cause that girl was so fine. I never had the courage to do no shit like that, but the hunger was growin' in me and I had to try it. See Roshawn was the only girl I had ever wanted to even consider doing that with, at the time. I think it was her carmel colored skin that had me buggin' or maybe it was when my uncle told me, lil nigga— to eat her is to keep her.

I remember the day it happened, one day at school a usual skip day, I ran into Roshawn around third hour at her locker.

"Ay, Roshawn."

"What's up baby."

"What's up with you after school today?"

"Shit."

"Then peep this, Let's go over Terrell's crib."

"Well I was intendin' on leaving after fifth hour, cause my sixth hour teacher ain't gonna be there."

"Bet, we can buss up after fifth hour it a give me more time to chill with you."

"Alright then meet me after fifth hour here at my locker."

"Bet."

Fifth hour, I loved being in there that was my english class that year and my teacher was Mrs. Evans. She was like my second momma and you bet not say anything out the way to Mrs. Evans. Cause a nigga fuckin' with Mrs. Evans was fuckin' with us, the student's in her class and that meant we had to fuck you up. See she cared about us and we cared about her. She would let us have fun but she would also get right in yo' ass quick and put you in yo' place. I kept good grades in her class cause she made a nigga want to learn. Other teachers just threw shit in yo' face and told you to do it, but Mrs. Evans would be like don't sit there and act like you know what's goin on and you really don't. If you have a problem tell me now so we can deal with it right now. Plus she would talk to you, learn you as a person. You could go and talk to her about anything and she would listen. She knew how to be fun but serious with us, and we like that. I think the one main reason we all was so cool with Mrs. Evans she was like your momma in school. You could run to her when you was in trouble, or when you just needed somebody to talk to, and we loved her for that.

After class I headed for the four hundreds cause that's where Roshawn's locker was at. When I got there she was putting her books in the locker and gettin' her starter jacket out. She loved the mutha' fuckin' Michigan Wolverine's, shid I can't lie, them my nigga's too. She had a gold wolverine starter, I mean the bright one and it was sweet, but I like the blue one cause I'm a dark color ass nigga, ya know. She always bought her jackets extra large so I could wear it and so it could droop half-way over her ass. I know my baby like a book and to this day she still the same way.

"You ready girl?"

"Hell yeah, just let me git my english folder."

"Ay we gonna walk down Van Dyke to the Caniff bus stop. Alright?"

"Why?"

"I was gonna buy you somethin' at the Sandwich Place."

"Oh hell yeah! I ain't had shit to eat all day."

"What'chu want?"

"I don't know, what ever."

"Man you better decide what you want by the time we get there."

"I will, I will."

Leaving out the building was some shit, cause all the doors were locked except the one's in the front, and that's where the security guards sat at. Mrs. Powell was always cuttin' a nigga up quick wit some old smart ass shit.

"Yall to lazy to keep your little hot behinds in school a whole day."

"No Mrs. Powell we just got to go home, it's important."

"Important my ass, yall ain't goin' no where important. Yall just think ya' to damn smart to stay in school and learn something."

"Whatever you say Mrs. Powell."

"I know it's whatever I say, yall ain't going no where important, how many times have I heard that imortant shit."

"Who you think...!"

"Don't say nothin' Roshawn let's just go and do our thang."

"She ain't gonna be cussin' at me!"

"I know baby, I know but ain't no need to git kicked out of school over no bullshit."

"She gonna git hers, she keep fuckin' wit me!"

Mrs. Powell was crazy as fuck. She a start cussin' at yo ass quick, and she didn't care what you said. I guess she loved to argue or somethin' cause she would go blow for blow against the best of them. She was cool sometimes but what really made us mad with her was the fact that she could tell when you was lying in a minute. It's like she made all the game in the world, I don't know— fuck it.

The Sandwich Place was on the corner of Van Dyke and Harper right by the Men's Wear. Soon as we walked past it, I looked in and before I could say anything."

"Damn you see that?"

"What?"

As if I didn't know.

"That Michigan Polo. I gotta' have that."

"Hell yeah, we both need to see one."

"On the real baby, damn it's sweet as fuck."

"Yes, but we better hurry up and git this sandwich before we fuck around and miss that bus, and you know how that damn Caniff bus run."

"Alright, let's go."

"Na what do you want?"

"Um! Gimme that grilled cheese with ham, like we had the other day and a large orange juice."

"Anything else?"

"Nope, nothin' at all."

"Ay Mr. Rositti one grilled cheese with ham, one chilli fries with cheese, and two large orange juices to go."

"Ay Marcel, hi ya doin'?"

"I'm cool Mr. Rositti, just chillin'."

"You kids and your funny talk. That will be $5.90 Marcel."

"Thanks Mr. Rositti."

"You kids have a good one."

"Mos def."

"Come on girl we don't want to miss that damn Caniff."

"Hell yeah, cause that bitch slow as fuck."

The Caniff usually got to Van Dyke around 1:42p.m. and it was already 1:35p.m. and we still had to walk around the bend to Miller. We got there just in time, hopped on the bus quick as fuck.

"You know you can't eat on the bus."

"Ah yeah we know."

"Alright."

The bus driver always got somethin' to say.

"Where you gonna sit at?"

"Let's go to the back."

"Hell naw! That's to far, let's sit right by the back door cause we about to git off in a minute."

When we use ta' ride the bus we would just lay on each other and chill, and anyway— the sound of the bus engine ah' damn near put yo ass to sleep."

"How far we gotta' go?"

"Shid we gonna git off when we past that light up there, so be ready to hit the bell."

"Okay just say when."

"Right about— now."

My cousin Terrell lived on Doremus, and that nigga ain't never go to school. Auntie Linda worker at Clayton Motors and didn't git home until around six or seven o'clock. So Terrell never had to worry about gittin' caught when he was skippin' school. He already had two kids and wasn't nothin' but seventeen years old. That nigga was wild and didn't give a fuck. When we got there dat nigga was gone.

"Damn this nigga ain't even here!"

"Open the screen door and knock, I know sometimes at my house we can't hear if you knock on the screen door."

"Hell yeah, Damn look, a piece of paper, that nigga can't even tape a note to the door."

"What it say?"

Marcel if you git here before I git back just wait. I went to drop my daughter off and I'll be right back.

"Does his daughter live far from here?"

"Naw, she live on Six Mile and Gable. Right acros the bridge. Shid we a just wait a minute."

"Gimme my sandwich."

"Uh-Uh, hold on a minute damn you ain't starvin'."

"Nigga you don't know what my stomach feels like, na gimme my damn sandwich!"

"No man, wait a minute."

"You make my ass sick!"

"Whatever."

Once again I was fuckin' with her just to see her eyes when she got mad. She a start rollin' her head and cuttin' her eyes and damn I loved to see that shit. For the first time I could actually say that the feelin' that I was feelin' was love. My life, I lived as a thug slash student and fast than a bitch. I wanted to be a thug nigga sellin' weed makin' fast money, but then wanted to git my education so I wouldn't be a dumb ass nigga, and she was my heart. One day I was gonna let her know about my life but until then I was gonna stack and keep her next to me.

"Is this yo cousin, comin' up the block?"

"Hell yeah, come on. What up nigga?"

"Shit, just chillin'."

"Ay, this my girl Roshawn, and this is my cousin Terrell."

"What up."

"Nothin, and do you have a friend?"

"Didn't you just leave your baby momma's house."

"Look baby I'm a scorpio and I need as much as I can get."

"So you just a freak."

"Born for the purpose, baby and lovin' every minute of it."

We walked into the crib and sat down on the couch in the front room.

"Roshawn here eat your sandwich."

"Gimme some ice for my juice."

"Alright."

And as I went into the kitchen with Terrell I set up the activity for the day.

"Ay yo Terrell I need to use your room dog."

"Ain't no thang my nigga, just change my sheets."

"Bet, you want some of these chilli fries?"

"Cheese on them?"

"Mos def, I wouldn't eat'um any other way."

"Hell yeah gimme some, just put'um on a plate and sit'um in the icebox."

"Bet."

When I walked back in the front room with the ice I gave it to her and sat down next to her.

"Here your ice."

"Thank you, na you know I got to be home by five o'clock."

"I know when you gotta' be at the crib, shid it ain't nothin' but three o' three, we got plenty of time."

"I'm just lettin' you know."

"Mmmm hmmm, my baby gonna' give some lovin' today."

"Move."

"Come here, gimme some love girl."

"Boy you play so much."

"I'm a lick you all over."

"Lick me all over."

"Believe that, all over."

"I got's to see this."

"Oh you will see, let's go upstairs."

Takin' Roshawn upstairs to the bedroom, a usual routine at my house, but this time in Terrell's room she is gonna' git a suprise. My cousin had his room made up into a sex palace. That nigga had every R&B song on the radio. A fat-ass bed and a dog ass system. Roshawn had set on the bed while I was fuckin' wit the CD's. She liked hearin' some Keith Sweat, so I popped his CD in and sat down next to her. With my hand up under her shirt we started kissin'. Her lips was so soft and sweet I couldn't git enough. To this day I love fuckin' her, cause she knows how to fuck. She pulled my shirt up and started kissin' and suckin' on my nipples. Then I pulled out a fat-ass blunt and we both smoked and kissed till it was gone. She stood up and started takin' off her clothes, and then I layed her body down on the bed. I touched them with my tongue, flickin' her nipples with the tip she licked that. In my head all I could think about was that crazy shit that my uncle use to tell me about, and on the real it didn't seem to crazy no more lookin' at Roshawn's body. I intended to use all that shit on her, this particular day. I attacked her nipples like a beast, she moaned and moved around like she couldn't take it. I licked her down to her belly and kissed her on her waist. She looked up in suprise that I had went so low, cause I had never went down that far before, I had to go all the way. I kissed her down her legs across her feet and sucked every toe, damn she was lovin' it. All this time I thought my uncle was talkin' crazy shit, eat the pussy. Damn I kissed her back up her leg's and then pushed her leg's up and spead them apart. Nigga what, it wasn't nothin' like I thought. That shit was good as hell no lie, and she was lovin' it my nigga fo-real. She was squirmin' and screamin' in a low tone, my name like I had never heard it before. The next thing I knew she was shakin' like a damn crazy mutha' fucka' pullin' and jerkin', grabbin'

me and pullin' me up on top of her. Kissin' me like she tryin' to lick her juices from around my mouth, and I was lovin' the shit. Out of the blue and unprepared for what was about to happen next, I watched her pull my jeans down. She damn near tore my mutha fuckin' boxer's off. My nigga she started lickin' all around my dick, I was like damn but when she put the head of my dick in her mouth, my nigga she took sheer control of every sense of touch in my body. My eye's rolled to the back of my head as she swirled her mouth around my dick. Up and down, my Lord! Never in my sixteen years on this earth had I felt anything so good. I could feel her suckin' my deepest passions out through my ball's, and was helplessly overwhelmed by her as I exploded so uncontrollably. Then within an instant she leaped up on top of me and rode me like a black stallion in rough terraine. My dick was hurtin' from risin' and goin' down at the same time and her pussy muscle squeezin' my shit.

Her head swayed back and forth, side to side and I was going out of my mind as our bodies collided like waves everytime we hit each other passionately. Once again we explode like two volcano's, never had cummin' inside her felt so good. We layed there for a minute and held each other in amazement at what we had just done, it was incredible.

"Nigga, what time is it?"

"Damn where my pager at? Damn where my pager at? Hmmm hear you go right here, it is four thirty-one."

"Shit I got's to go home."

"Where your panties at?"

"Over there, you think your cousin a drive me home?"

"Hell yeah he droppin' us both off."

"Ask him can I use the phone?"

"Hold on."

As I got up and put my shit on, I went to the door and called Terrell.

"Ay Terrell! Terrell!"

Hollin' for that nigga down stairs.

"What up."

"Let me see that wire for a minute?"

"Hold up, let me get it."

"Alright, he goin' to get it."

"Who you callin'?"

"My house."

"Well look, go down stairs and let T' give you the phone while I change these sheets."

"Alright."

She went on down the stairs as I changed the sheets and straightened up for my nigga, then I went downstairs. When I got down there Roshawn was sittin' on the couch.

"Did you call home?"

"Hell yeah my daddy ain't came over yet."

"Shid then we up out of here, ay T' we ready!"

"Alright my nigga, I'll be outside in a minute."

"Yeah."

While on the porch standing for a minute, Roshawn had walked down to the car. I was still tryin' to believe the shit we had just done. It was unbelievable, then the door opened.

"Hop in the ride my nigga' we out."

"Hell yeah."

"Now where your girl live at?"

"She live around the corner from me, my nigga on the corner."

"You ain't got no trees on you?"

"Look in the glove box."

"Ah shit my nigga this what I'm talkin' bout. Where you git this at?"

"Over on Evaline."

"Hell yeah them nigga's be havin' the funk."

"Shid spark that bitch up."

"You gonna' hit this Roshawn?"

"I might takc a couple of puffs."

"Then gimme that lighter."

"This the mutha' fuckin' green's nigga, I'm tellin' you."

"That's the only place I go to in the hood."

By the time we got to my hood we were only half way finished with the blunt. So Terrell parked at the end of my block and continue blowin', then my pager went off.

"Who is that?"

"Corn."

"Let me see?"

"For what?"

"Cause I want to see."

"Here look, thinkin' I'm lyin' and shit."

"I didn't say you was."

"But you thought so."

"Well on that note I got's to go home."

"You not gonna' finish the blunt?"

"Nope, I got's to go home."

"You gonna' call me tonight?"

"Yeah when I come home from bein' wit my Daddy."

"Naw I'll walk, I ain't no where but round the corner."
"You my boo?"
"Yeah."
"Gimme a kiss?"
Her lip's felt so damn good, I ain't wanna' stop kissin' her.
"Ah-ight, I'll talk to you tonight."
"Ay nigga you ready to git dropped off?"
"Hell yeah, but drop me off on Woodlawn at the spot."
"Bet."

****

Day Two

Woodlawn was the spot baby. Weed 24/7 everyday, the fattest, greenest of tree's in the D, and from 5:30 to 8:45 that was my house. It was day's when I sat up in there and made $400 in three hours. When I first started I was a fifteen year old nigga sittin' in school wit C-notes in my pocket. I was lovin' the shit, everything about the shit was hype then a bitch. If my Momma would'a knew the shit I use to do I swear she'd a beat the shit out of me. I use ta' let loose on nigga's quick, throwin' bullet's at soft ma'fucka's like it wasn't shit. A young thug nigga makin' money and livin' the life. I would blow so much cheese drinkin' and partyin' or buyin' clothes and bluntin'um up it was ridiculus. The game was showin' me gee's and I was gonna make it.

"Ah-ight my nigga, I'll hit you up tommorrow."

"Mos-def."

Everytime I was up in that bitch it was hype. It was Javon's spot, the nigga that live's downstairs from me and that nigga was real as hell. You come to the door, you git yo shit and leave. At night, cut yo light's off and turn yo' music down and he didn't play. Have yo' money out and ready when you hit the street, and be nonchalant about yo' shit. He use to talk to a nigga' all the time, he looked after me and Momma and Tamika cause we ain't have no father. It wasn't like he was tryin' to be our daddy or nothin' but he just knew my Momma was alone payin' the rent and raising us and he liked to see that. He sometimes called my Momma his Momma and he didn't let nobody fuck wit us. See his Momma died when he was ten and his Daddy died when he was seventeen, so he has never really had a family. He did talk about his little sister Briana, she was sixteen then an she had everything cell, pager, gear and money. She walked around her hood like the shit, Javon would always ask if we needed anything and if we did best believe he would git it. In the spot Javon would pull me to the side all the time and kick shit in my ear. He told me, this game is a bitch and it doesn't care about nothin' and nobody. You git in, git yo' shit, then git out.

Make yo' money and utilize the money so you a alway's have money. The day you let this game become your life, you gonna' lose your life and your soul. You do your thang and don't be out to cut a nigga in the game and you won't git cut. Although their are nigga's that won't play by the rule's so you have to be on your guard at all time's watching everything and everybody. Get an education cause you can't ball all your life, take yo' money and stack, put it to good use in some real shit where the law can't

fuck wit'chu and always in all you do, take God on your side. My Momma taught my that before she died, more than anything he'll always bring you home. The nigga was smart and he knew what he was doin', he use to tell me that I reminded him of himself and that's why he was schoolin' me. So how could I listen when my teachers was tellin' me not to associate with drug dealers, or look at those hoe-ass government commercials about this is your brain on drug's.

****

Fuck that, I ain't want to see that shit when this shit had put gee's in my pocket like nigga what. He never came on me without bein' real and I wanted to be like that nigga. I mean, I had seen that nigga do some scandelous shit and I also seen that nigga do some nice shit. So why would I go any other way. I remember when he told me that the game a bring you some good times and it a bring you some bad times. Just git yo' shit on, stack up ya' money and you a blow the fuck up. Nigga in this game you succeed only by bein' smart, alert, and persevere. Hungry none thinkin' ass nigga's rush into shit and git fucked up. Lookin' for nothin' but money and put all their feelin's and compassion to the side. Then he told me somethin' that stuck in my head to this day and I feel that I will remember this for the rest of my life. He told me, whatever you do, God is watchin' and he see's how it's goin' down. Don't let him see you down here fuckin' up and forgettin' who you are for this cheese. You give and let him give you more for your heart, not your blood thirsty hunger. I've never fucked with a mutha' fucka' who didn't fuck wit me.

We all had a sack, a quarter pound a piece, no more, no less. Until you run out. Four nigga's in the spot flippin' like a mutha' fucka'. He taught me how to save my money, I didn't have to buy tree's cause he would blaze about a hundred dolla's worth a day, and we smoked it wit him.

Corn would be crankin' like me but he would be blowin' his shit like a maniac. As fast as he got it, that's how fast he lost it. I tried to tell that nigga' the shit that Javon was tellin' me but he wouldn't listen to me, but I loved dat' nigga cause we had been together for a long, long time and dat' nigga is like a brother to me. Maybe one day that nigga will understand this shit and handle business and do that shit the right way. I wanted us to both blow up in that shit, but I fear my nigga ain't gonna' come up out that mindframe.

Javon for some reason saw me maturing in the game and runnin' my own shit, and when he get's out of it I'll be the nigga he give his empire to, and when that time would have came, I'd have been ready. One day he told me that once you go through all the painful bullshit of the game you might

as well keep going cause the rewards of persistance are the only things left to ease your mind.

That night time was movin' fast, it was already eight twenty-four and Javon hadn't come in yet. I really had to holla' at him, my mid-term was comin' up and if 1 would have failed my Momma would have beat the shit outta' me— I had to be ready.

"Ay Calil is Javon comin' through today?"

"I don't know my nigga' cause I ain't seen that nigga all day."

"Corn, page that nigga."

"Hold up let me finish addin' this money up."

Beep-Beep-Beep-Beep

"Who the fuck, damn it's Roshawn, I can't call her back from here. I'm a have to wait till I git to the crib."

****

"Ay nigga', I paged Von. He should be callin' back in a minute."

"Bet."

Ring-Ring-Ring-Ring

"Hello."

"What up."

"Von, whad up. This Cell."

"Whad up, my nigga'."

"When you comin' through? I need to holla' at you."

"I'll be through there in about fifteen minutes."

"Bet."

"Von on his way, he a be here in a few minutes."

"Geah."

So much shit was on my mind that it was hard to concentrate on any of the shit. My girl, my hustle, my school, my Momma, damn all at one time fuckin' wit my head. I was tryin' my best to put that shit in perspective but I couldn't. I had cheese stashed away so I didn't need none right then, but I was lovin' to make the money. I think I had enough to chill wit for that next couple of day's. Shid— fo-real I only needed about three day's of studyin' and that wasn't shit. It didn't take me long to study cause I knew my shit. I couldn't come home wit a fucked up report card, my Momma didn't play that shit. My Momma always told me and my sister, get your high school diploma and college was your own choice. So I felt like damn is that it, why would that be so hard for me to do for my Momma. hard as she worked to keep gear on us and a roof over our head's. I couldn't let my Momma down. two more years and I'd a had that bitch in my hand's. A fat-ass diploma, hangin' next to my Mommas' and my sisters' on the dinnin' room wall.

Some of them nigga's didn't give a fuck about school or graduatin', so they didn't worry about shit but gettin' money. I fucked around and skipped a lot of class, but my work got turned in. I knew math would alway's be my lowest grade on my report card.

Knock-Knock-Knock-

"Who is it?"

"Von."

"What up doe?"

"Everything straight?"

"Cel, what'chu wanna' holla' at me about?"

"A lil' somethin'."

"Well come on in here and holla' at me."

"I got mid-terms comin' up and I need about three day's to study."

"That's it my nigga', you know you ain't gotta' ask me about no shit like that. Nigga' what I tell you about yo' school work?"

****

"I know, I know my nigga'. I ain't say it like that, 1 was just lettin' you know I had to do some work and couldn't be here for a few day's."

"I hear ya' lil' nigga' whatever you gotta' do. How ya' people doin?"

"They straight."

"And what about my girl?"

"Momma, she tight."

"Bet, how much you git off today?"

"A Q-P."

"Let me git that, this yours and here a little somethin' extra, git them grades right."

"Alright Von, I'm out."

"Holla' at me later my nigga'."

"Mos-def."

So when you tell me that all drug dealer's are bad. I couldn't feel that bullshit. That nigga' Von took care of a nigga'. I looked up to that nigga' and everythang he did. Damn but I had a bigger problem, what to tell Roshawn about why I didn't call her back when she paged me. She use to swear I was out wit some bitch. Von said bitches and hustlin' didn't mix. When you stackin' you can't have a main bitch, they only do three things. Keep your mind cluttered with a bunch a bullshit, make you spend your doe, or set you up. I use to have to pray to God that Tamika ass wasn't on the phone.

"Where the hell have you been at?"

"Momma what'chu mean?"

"Where the fuck have you been boy?"

"I was, I was..."

"Don't you lie to me boy, don't make me beat'cho ass."

"I was over Terrell's house then I went over Roshawn's house."

"Why did your teacher call here and say you been skippin'?"

"I don't know!"

"What you mean you don't know, don't raise your voice at me Marcel! I will kick your mutha' fuckin' ass up in here do you hear me?"

"Yes."

"Excuse me!"

"Yes Momma."

"Don't let me hear this shit again, cause I will hurt you boy. Go to your room, I don't want to see your face."

Stompin' into the room was my motto, nigga' what. She was alway's trippin'.

"Don't stomp on my floor, I don't know what the fuck your problem is!"

My Momma, you gotta' love her but she was quick to start flippin', I didn't understand sometimes where her head was at. I couldn't talk to my Momma about certain shit, I would git nervous. It's something about my Momma I tell you that I just can't figure out to this day. Around her I'm always wonderin' how does she see me in her eye's what does she be thinkin' when she look's at me. I just didn't want to fail in her eye's ya' know, I wanted to make her happy and buy her a lot of shit, so I hustled so my shit could be tight until I reached the next level.

Sittin' in my room like damn I couldn't call Roshawn and knew I was gonna hear some shit when I got to school the next day.

Beep-Beep-Beep-Beep

And there she went again, fuck I knew it was over then. She was gonna' be clowin' and I would be ready to knock the fuck out of her. Fuck it, I decided to go to the library the next day and study, I had to do it anyway so I'll be gettin' started up then.

That next mornin' was wild cause it started off chill and layed back but you never knew what to expect within the hour's of the day. This world I'm tellin' you, as I woke up to the sweet smell of burnin' green was so good to me. Von was downstair's doin' his thang and I was out to go and handle my shit for that day. Life was great for the most part, I was gonna' git good grade's on my mid-term's and look straight glossy in front of Momma and have her off my back for the rest of the semester. I ain't no fool I knew how to put my business first cause I knew I'd have plenty of time to the main library on Woodward, sometimes I couldn't believe how hype it was up in the library. All those Wayne State bitches was really lookin' good. I think that my life was just flyin' by sometimes when I just remenisce, the type of

shit I thought about and the image's that floated through my head— it happen's now when I'm just thinkin'. Use to wonder about makin' it erase frequently. My one true constant was the thought of my Momma havin' shit and my nigga's, Von made us that way.

"Shit my stop."

A nigga use to fuck around and miss the bus thinkin' about some wild shit, shit I do to this day thinkin' to hard. Damn I saw so many bad ass bitches in there that day, it was alway's new bad bitches in the library. Made it so hard to focus on your studies, I started with my science shit just to knock it out the way. I think I hated that more than I did math. The periodic table, man I'm never gonna' use that shit in real life, well not my life. My job was hustla' slash thug until it was time to move on. Fuck-naw I couldn't believe it was that many elements, until.

"Excuse me?"

"Ay! Whad'up."

"May I tell you something?"

"Whatever you want."

"You have some very pretty lip's."

"Thank you."

"Can I sit here?"

"Go head."

******

"My name is Diana."

"I'm Marcel."

"What school do you go to?"

"Kettering."

"You in high school?"

"Yeah, ain't you."

"Naw I go to WC3."

"How old are you?"

"I'm nineteen."

"Damn, fo-real?"

"Yeah."

"Guess how old I am?"

"I don't know, around seventeen."

"Sixteen and 3/4th."

"Git the fuck outta' here."

"Fo-real."

"Oh my God! I'm attracted to a young ass nigga'."

"Don't let that fool you baby, it ain't my fault I had a beard and a mustache at fifteen. Ol' Cel a flex yo' lil' pretty ass."

"Boy I could hurt you."

"I would really beg to differ."

"Evidently enough to attract you to me

"True dat, I can't argue wit dat, you got me."

"So what else made you come see me besides my lip's."

"Your eye's."

"That's it?"

"Mmmmm Hmmmm."

"So what up, where your man at?"

"I don't have one."

"You got a friend?"

"Somewhat."

"What dat mean?"

"It mean's I got a friend."

"And if I didn't want to be your friend?"

"And who said you had to be?"

"So what'chu sayin'?"

"In time we a see."

"So you wanna' kick it wit a nigga'?"

"I ain't sayin' nothin'."

"Well gimme yo' phone number."

"Why

****

"So I can call you later and show you where my head is at."

"Mmmmm."

"What?"

"`I'm scared of you."

"Don't be, it ain't no need to be afraid, I ain't gonna' hurt you baby foreal."

"You talkin' some mad shit, I'm a see where your head at."

"So write that number down and let me show you."

"Here hit me up later."

"Bet, no thang baby I'm a hit you up around nine/nine-thirty

"Nine/nine-thirty tonight, bet."

"Alright."

"I'll be hittin' you up."

Female's, boy I tell ya' it's alway's gold to keep your game tight, hollin' at the honies, shid it's alway's good to let loose with mad game kickin'.

Beep-Beep-Beep-Beep

Damn what the fuck, I thought in my mind as I looked down at my pager. Who the fuck callin' me knowin' I'm handlin' my biz. This shit better be important I thought as I lifted it from my waist to my eye's. It was my crib so I got up and walked to the pay phone. I knew it wasn't my Momma cause she was at work, so it had to be my sister.

Ring-Ring-Ring-Ring

"Hello."

"Who dis?"

"Tamika."

"Oh! whad'up, and what's wrong with your voice?"

"Marcel, where you at?"

"I'm at the library. Why?"

"You gotta' come home quick."

"Why? Whad'up?"

"Terrell got killed!"

"What! You bullshitin'? Stop lyin' to me."

"I'm not bullshittin', Marcel come home now!"

"I'm on my way!"

I couldn't believe that shit, Terrell dead what kind of shit was that. I wished I could have turned back the hands of time to before that day. That shit had fucked wit a nigga mind all the way back to the hood, one day he there with a nigga the next day he wasn't. I knew Auntie had fell out, it wasn't no going around that shit. All the little bitches he was fuckin' wit, he had them hoes in love with him. I didn't know if Roshawn knew or not but I knew I had to tell her. Damn I didn't even think about his kid's until half way home, that was the worst part of all. I knew them kid's loved they Daddy.

Fuck, I had started thinkin' so hard I didn't even realize I had started cryin'. What the hell is the world comin' to, I thought as I looked out of the bus window lookin' at the world and at people's faces. Mad as fuck cause I knew they didn't feel the pain that I was feelin'. I hated the fact that they could just sit there and not feel nothin' about the death of my cousin but shit they didn't know him. I wanted them too maybe feel what I felt, thinkin' that would have eased my mind, but after I thought again it wouldn't have helped at all.

My street was packed with people but shit it felt so empty I couldn't feel the usual happy feelin' to be on my street. The talkin' and laughin' even that that was towards me felt incomplacent and seemed to go right through me. My mutha' fuckin' world was so hollow I didn't know what to do. My crib had a dark feelin' over it I mean you really had to look at it to see it, but my heart was worn down and my house was filled with gloom and just maybe

that was that grey cloud over my crib that only I could see. My sister rushed to the door when I opened it.

"Momma, Momma is that you?"

"Naw it's me, Tamika."

She grabbed me cryin' and I couldn't do shit but stand there and hold her. Death is nothin' but pain, hurt, and lose and when you got an emotional family like mine that shit doubles. I didn't know wether to say somethin' or just stand there and hold her, but see that's a rare time to see my sister all broke down emotionally and not pushin' me around in her own way, but I knew that wasn't shit compared to how my Momma was gonna' act when she got to the crib. It was really fucked up when she got home. Every picture, every plate, every noise reminded her of that boy, she was fallin' out and cryin'. It was a very depressing day in our household and I had to git out and do somethin' so I wouldn't fall into the same shit. So I left and went around to the spot and got blowed till I couldn't see shit and fell out.

****

Day Three

Beep-Beep-Beep-Beep

I remember that beeper alarm like it was yesterday. Wakin' up out of a deep ass dream, I believe I was dreamin' about Terrell when I woke up. I can't remember what we were doing but I do recall seeing his face. I got up and gazed out the window at the morning sky, I guess God was comin' to the funeral today with us cause the grey cold sky was filled with wind and rain like he was cryin', or maybe that's just what I was hopin' he was doin'. So I got up and headed to the kitchen to get somethin' to drink. I walked past my sister's room it was the one in front of mine, I looked in at her sleepin'. I realized that life was short and fast so hold tight to that that you have in your possession. She looked so pretty layin' there, I can still see the tear stain's runnin' down her face from cryin' all that night. I just put my head down and closed the door then walked to the kitchen. When I opened the icebox I grabbed the juice jug and started drinkin' it right out the bottle. Momma said don't drink out the bottle and if she'd a caught me she would have fucked me up, but it was a habit that me and my sister did all the time. As I titled my head back I felt a cold breeze walked up my neck so I turned to see where it was comin' from. I looked through the dinnin' room to the front room windows but they were shut. So I walked up to the front room and looked at the upstairs porch and the door was wide open. When I looked out and saw my Momma just standin' their in her housecoat cryin'. Her bottom lip was shakin' and she was tremblin' like she was freezin'.

"Momma are you alright?"

She was silent as she looked up into the sky and took a deep breath.

"Huh-huh— Oh Marcel, what are you doing up this early for baby?"

"Momma, it's 8:15 in the mornin'. I been up and couldn't go back to sleep. Are you all right?"

"Probably when this day is over with. Is your sister woke yet?"

"No."

"What are you doing with that juice jug? Did you drink out that jug again? I am gonna' hurt you and your sister about that."

"It wasn't nothin' but a little in it Momma."

"Don't leave that bottle on the table when your finished, and wake your sister up so she can get ready for this funeral."

"Ok Momma."

When I went to wake Tamika up she didn't git up as her usual self, all grouchy and shit. She sat up in her bed and just started cryin' all over again from last night.

"I don't wanna' go. I don't wanna' see him in that casket, Mar-Mar."

I couldn't do shit but sit there and hold her. She hadn't called me Mar-Mar since I was ten, her and Momma was the only one's that ever called me that and the only one's that ever will. Then I said to her.

"It's alright Mika, he in a better place."

That was all I could think of to say and in a way it was true. No more pain and hurt for him, but it was tearin' us here apart.

"Momma said we gotta' git ready. She out on the porch, I guess she gonna' wait til we git ready first."

"Alright let's go see how she doin' first."

As we got up and walked out of her room I'll never forget she turned to me and said.

"Mar-Mar, I love you. We don't say it enough to each other but I'm a start now."

It blew me away, my sister and me showin' this kind of deep emotion to each other.

"I love you to Mika."

Then she went out on the porch with Momma as I started back to my room. When I got there I just layed on my bed thinkin' damn this shit done sparked a fire in us that wasn't there last week. I mean we said I love you before to each other, but never this deep and meaningful. I saw my sister in a whole new light it's like I alway's saw her as a mean big sister tellin' on me and bullyin' me around cause she was the oldest, but then I saw her all emotional.

When I heard the bathroom water runnin' I knew she was in there gettin' ready, so I went to my closet and got my black funeral suit out and layed it on the bed when the phone rung. I listened to hear my Momma pick it up but she didn't so I ran into the dinnin' room to get it.

"Hello?"

"Marcel, what time is your Mother comin' over here?"

"Roshawn what'up doe, we should be comin' over there about nine."

"Alright, so how you holdin' up? You think you can take it?"

"I'm straight for now."

"Are you Sure?"

"Yeah I'm sure, but I don't know how I'm a feel when I see him."

"Me neither."

"Look I'll see you in a lil' bit."

"Alright, bye-bye boo."

"Bye-bye."

Before I could hang up the phone and turn around it rung again.

"Hello?"

"Marcel, is that you?"

"Hi Gra-ma."

"Where your Mother at?"

****

"On the porch."

"Tell her we in Detroit, and we'll meet her at the funeral home."

"Gra-ma I didn't know you was comin'."

"You better believe I was comin' and I'm over your uncle Terrell's house."

"Ok Gra-ma, love you."

"Love you to baby."

When I hung up I went straight to the porch.

"Momma."

"What?"

"Gra-ma here, she over uncle Terrell's house. She said she gonna' meet us at the funeral home."

"Alright, and why ya'll ain't dressed. Ya'll better hurry up it's already 8:35."

"We comin' Momma."

I went and put my gear on and called my sister.

"Mika are you ready yet?"

"Yeah I'm ready."

When we went to git Momma and get in the car Momma said somethin' mind-bogglin'.

"Mika when we git Linda's house I'm gonna' ride in the family car and you gonna' go pick up Roshawn and yall come straight to the funeral home. Do you hear me?"

"Yes Momma."

The ride felt like eternity, everybody was silent and still just lookin' forward. When we pulled up to Auntie Linda's house it didn't look the same. It had a horrible gloom to it, you could see the pain and loss all around it. A limo was in front of the house, Momma didn't even park, she just stopped in the middle of the street and got out and let Mika get the wheel. I was in the backseat and just stayed there waiting for Roshawn to git in. I knew that she was going to need somebody to hold her cause her and Terrell was tight. When we pulled up in front of her house I told Mika to blow the horn. It was 9:14 and Roshawn came out in this bad ass dress. I felt a little ashamed cause this was a funeral we were going to and she for a

moment made me think about her body as she walked down the walk way. I rolled the window down and said git in the back.

"Your Momma lettin' you drive the car Mika?"

"Hell yeah, and we only got twenty-two minutes to get to the funeral home. What's the quickest way to Blvd. and Mack?"

"You might as well go straight down Van Dyke to Mack and you a be right there."

"Then let's go before Momma think we was bullshittin'."

"I can't believe Terrell gone, Marcel."

"I know this shit trippin' me out."

****

She leaned over and laid her head on my chest and stayed that way until we pulled up to the funeral home. It was hard as hell to find a parking space that day, I think it was a couple of funeral's that day all at the same time or somethin'. Nothin' prepared me for the scene over that boy's casket when I walked in and saw Auntie Linda fallin' out. Momma was no help for her cause she was next to her doin' the same thing. Uncle Terrell, who Terrell was named after was tryin' to console both of them but he wasn't takin' it that well his damn self. Gra-ma was just cryin', she wasn't loosin' it like the rest of them but his two baby momma's were clownin'. Tyler the Momma of his first baby Sherry, had fell on the floor and started shakin'. While Monica his second baby Danisha's Momma was just yellin' for that nigga' to come back, she was in love with him. I walked up to the casket me and Roshawn and we just put our heads down. In my head I was tellin' dat nigga I'm a find the bitch ass nigga' that done this shit to him. I was gonna' kill that nigga' fo-real. The hunger that brought out of me at that moment had me ready to kill somethin' quick. I felt like damn, look at all the pain some bitch nigga' done caused me and my people. We didn't need to be here today doin' this. We could have been chillin' but no— some hoe nigga' had to do some dumb shit. Now I gotta' see somebody about this matter in the worst way, was all I was thinkin'.

By the time we got to Uncle Terrell's house my Momma had cooled down and was comin' back round to Momma in her normal mind. Everytime after a funeral we went over somebodies house and ate like we didn't give a fuck about throwin'-up. Momma had started makin' plates and makin' people do stuff like they was at home. She was the oldest and everybody listened to her. The only one over her was Gra-ma and she mostly chilled and let Momma run thangs. See Momma was forty-one, Uncle Terrell was thirty-eight, Auntie Linda was thirty-seven, and Auntie Renee was Twentynine. Uncle Terrell was the only boy and that's why Terrell was

named after him. I was sittin' in the front room of the house with my little sister on my lap. I usually didn't see her through the week cause she stayed over Auntie Renee's house while Momma was workin'. Auntie Renee had two kids then Reggie and Diana and they were around Kara's age so she had somebody to play with. As I sat there with her on my lap listenin' and lookin' at my family I heard Gra-ma talkin' to Auntie Linda tellin' her that God had Terrell and that he was in a better place. Hell that didn't do nothin' for me, I wanted to see my nigga' right here not in a better place. Shit the only thing bringin' any relief to the madness was the thought of seein' the nigga' who did this, dead and gone.

****

Day Four

For monthes the question beat my mutha' fuckin' head down. Who was that nigga'? I wanted him so bad that I could taste revenge in my drippin' sweat. I was obsessed by the thought handlin' that nigga'. Then when tips came my way through the courtesy of the streets, my lust was about to be fullfilled. My nigga' Corn was at the spot one day when a nigga' who be coppin' from us who lived around Mack and Conners told my nigga' he had a kat that lived his way wit some chrome deez for sale that would fit nicely on his 85' Capris. So Corn said bring the nigga' through, but the nigga' said that he'd rather take Corn over his way than bring the nigga' to the spot cause he didn't run wit him like that. Corn went over there the next day and saw the deez and froze up. The deez he was lookin' at was the deez he rode on so many times in my cousin's car. He bought the deez cash out and went straight to the crib and called me and told me to come over as quick as possible. From the tone in his voice I knew that it was some major shit. I had never heard the tremblin' in his voice like I heard right then. When I got to his crib he was cryin' and led me to the basement and then he said nigga' who use to ride on these. I just stood there lookin' at them, I can't even tell you what was goin' through my head at that moment. I was mad, I was sad, I was glad.

"My nigga' where you git these at?"

"You know who they belong to don't you?"

"Corn where did you git'em?"

"My nigga' who's are they?"

"I know who's they are, nigga' where did you git'em?"

"From dis hoe ass nigga' on Mack and Conners."

"What's da' nigga' name?"

"The nigga' name Reese."

"He over there on Mack and Conners nigga' that's his hood."

"What street he live on?"

"He live on Harding."

"On my way back I asked the nigga' to put me up on the deez, where the nigga' Reese git'em at and he told me the nigga' been ridin'em for about five monthes. An he the type a nigga' that a jack a nigga' all like that. A lil' gun happy young nigga'."

"We ridin' on this nigga' Corn tommorrow night."

"I feel you my nigga' just say the word when you ready."

The next day I fuck the shit out of Roshawn. Fucked her like I never fucked her before. I put so many nuts up in her that I thought she was gonna' bust. Then I paged Corn and had him meet me at Roshawn's house. When he got there we headed straight to the spot and got my nine. I cleaned the finger prints off the gun and bullets while Corn cleaned his Tech just in case we had to throw'em. We put our gloves on and hit the liquor store and had a crackhead go in and git us a half-a-pint of Hennessy. We sat in the parkin' lot and smoked a fat ass blunt and drunk the pint straight till it was damn near empty then we rolled out. Headed for the nigga' beatin' Shiyon P. and ready for some shit. All I had in my head was I'm out for this nigga' he done brought stress and grief to my life and I was gonna' make that nigga' pay wit his life. That's all I could see.

"Bring it to ya' face, nigga rewind that shit."

"Hell yeah, damn here that nigga' street right here."

"Nope, I can see from here he ain't there, but damn that car comin' down the block looks' like his shit."

As the car came closer I looked hard at it. My nigga' Corn looked close at the driver.

"Is that that nigga' Corn?"

"Hell yeah, let's turn around and ride back through."

"Nigga' when we ride back through I'm gonna' start straight bussin' at these nigga's."

"Whatever comes, comes my nigga'."

As we rode back up the block, like any nigga' in the streets the mu' fucka' was on alert starin' us down as we got closer. As soon as we got right up on him we just came out firin'. The bullets cracked through the silence as the nigga' jumped down for cover. He started to fire back I could hear the bullets tear the driver side up. I was sittin' on the passenger door shootin' at that nigga' wit no remorse. Then his boys ran out from eveywhere lettin' round's off like a scandelous beast, I took one in the shoulder and when I leaned back still firin' I hit one nigga' in the face. We scald off and his boy's was still bussin' at us down the block. One of them hoe ass nigga's blew the back tire out. We knew the cops was comin' so we was gonna' ditch the ride and make a run for it. We was goin' as fast as we could to find somewhere to jump out at when we went through a red light on Mack and got hit by a car. The car swerved around and hit the light pole I was damn near knocked out but I shook some of that shit off. I looked over at Corn to tell him let's go, then I saw the nigga' head all fucked up. I was like damn my nigga' to, but I had to get away. It felt like the last hour of my life runnin' like crazy tryin' to find any where to hide, but this wasn't my hood and I was bleedin' like a mu' fucka'. The blood lose was fuckin' me up I was runnin' down dark alley's and I was startin' to fall out.

Then all I could remember was leapin' over a gate and fallin' down on the ground lookin' up at the sky prayin' to God not to let me die.

****

Day Five

Now here I sit in my sixth year of a ten to fifteen year sentence with a chance for parole in two more years. I call my Momma once a month and see what's goin' on in the hood. I miss doin' all the shit I use to do in the streets. This jail shit make a mutha' fucka' think about how wonderful it feels when you in the streets. Comin' and goin' as you please, all that shit is over with. The worst part about it is, Roshawn got pregnant the last time I fucked her, the day my world changed. I got a five year old daughter named Markeeda that I have never seen outside the bar's of this prision. I wasn't there to see her walk or talk and I'm sick about it. My Momma fell out when she heard what I had done and when they read the verdict in court she just fell back in her chair with a look on her face of sheer disappointment. I didn't even want to look at her and I believe she damn sure didn't want to look at me. I still hear her sayin'.

"Why did you take yourself away from me."

The only thing that keeps me goin' is the thought of my parole. I got a child to raise and a life to rebuild. You don't think about life until you lose it and when you got it you don't know what the fuck to do with it. I got my priorities straight now and plans for raisin' my daughter so she don't fuck up and put herself in some unneccessary shit like this. Cause I don't ever want my Momma to look at me the same way she did in that court room ever again, and I don't want to look at my daughter one day the way my Momma looked at me. You feel me.

About the Author

Shiyon Perriyon
Entered into the World: November 22, 1972
Under Constellation: Scorpio

The creation of Shiyon Perriyon those many years ago was the creation of living understanding. A wanderer of many live's and feeling's within the great multitude of emotion's and hope's. Torn between the righteousness of his soul and the God forsaken hungers of his flesh. Speaking the thought's out loud that everyone feel's but most yearn to understand. This world a place of turmoil and dispair, needing to feel the power of love and giving.

His mission started out as the speaker of the place he represent's the ghetto, but over the year's he has grew into the speaker of human life.

"My sole purpose is to represent the emotion's of human being's."

His vivid and clear outlook of life layed out so percise, just in reach of your mental conception let's you reminisce on the idea's of people you know and people you see. People you may have grew up with and in some case's maybe even yourself.

The Living Incantation of Black Life the first book by Shiyon Perriyon is a compilation of sharp soul cutting word's and phrase's. It span's across the plain of evolution, and dive's into the sea of creativity.

He has over 160 R&B song's written and was nominated for the Crystal Lyrical Award in 1998. He has been published in the International Library of Poetry, three time's.

He has a very interesting and refreshing look at black society in his vivid yet secluded vision. Shiyon Perriyon's work is powerful and compelling to read, as his word's captivate the meaning of metaphoric phrases within his hand picked scene's of black life

The mixture of street life and school life in his growing up accounts for his sometime's harsh look at reality, but he still seems to get his emotional and soul touched point across.

Published Poetry:
by the International Library of Poetry,
Fly Away: published in 1994
GOD: published in 1999 and 2000
by The Starlite Cafe on www.starlitecafe.com,
You, and only You, The Theory, Through this World (I): published in 2000

by Shiyon Perriyon on www.blackplanet.com. perriyon_bp,

In Me, A moment before lust, GOD, You, and only You: published in 2000

Nominated for Poem of the Year in 2000 for GOD, by The International Poets Society.

www.ingramcontent.com/pod-product-compliance
Ingram Content Group UK Ltd.
Pitfield, Milton Keynes, MK11 3LW, UK
UKHW041942190726
13854UKWH00004B/1742